The C.S.S. *Florida*

T0307939

The C.S.S. *Florida:*
Her Building and Operations

Frank Lawrence Owsley, Jr.

The University of Alabama Press

Tuscaloosa and London

First published in the United States of America in 1965 by the
University of Pennsylvania Press

Also published in the United Kingdom, India, and Pakistan by the
Oxford University Press, London, Bombay, and Karachi

New edition published in 1987 by The University of Alabama Press

Library of Congress Cataloging-in-Publication Data

Owsley, Frank Lawrence, 1928–
The C.S.S. Florida.

Reprint. Originally published: Philadelphia :
University of Pennsylvania Press, 1965.
Bibliography: p. 191
Includes index.
1. Florida (Cruiser) 2. Confederate States of America. Navy—
History. 3. United States—History—Civil War, 1861–1865—Naval
operations. I. Title. II. Title: CSS Florida.
E599.F6097 2003   973.7'57   86-19362
ISBN 0-8173-1281-1

British Library Cataloguing-in-Publication Data available.

Contents

Acknowledgements

THIS AUTHOR WISHES to express his appreciation to Auburn University for a research grant-in-aid which permitted him to complete this work. He wishes to thank Mrs. Judy B. Carroll and Mr. Elbert L. Huber of the National Archives, Washington, D.C., and Dr. James W. Patton of the University of North Carolina for their help. Valuable information and suggestions were furnished him by Mr. William E. Geoghegan and Dr. Phillip K. Lundeberg, both of the Smithsonian Institution, Washington, D.C., and Dr. William S. Hoole of the University of Alabama Library. This author is indebted to Mr. Seale Johnson for his wise counsel and to Miss Suzanne Gray for her assistance in preparing the maps and diagrams for this work. He also wishes to express his appreciation for their valuable aid and criticism to Professor Richard S. West, Jr., Dr. James B. Sellers, Mrs. Margaret K. Latimer, Mrs. Harriet C. Owsley, Dr. Thomas A. Belser, Jr., Mrs. Susan H. Findley, and to his wife, Dorothy S. Owsley.

Introduction

In the twenty-one years since *The C.S.S. Florida: Her Building and Operations* was first published, numerous other books and articles have been written concerning the Confederate Navy, several of which deal with the cruisers and their officers. Most of these, however, are about C.S.S. *Alabama. C.S.S. Florida: Her Building and Operations* remains the only scholarly work specifically written about this ship. Even when one considers the newer studies, most historians appear reluctant to recognize the value of cruiser warfare. Many students of naval history still insist that the Civil War was the last major conflict in which surface cruisers were used effectively. This view is based on the assumption that the invention of the radio rendered the surface raider entirely too vulnerable; its victims could broadcast their location, bringing about a swift pursuit and destruction of the raider. Also, perhaps, the emergence of the submarine ultimately overshadowed the surface raider, though this interpretation probably discounts too much the role of the surface ships.

Many years ago when this author was still in high school, he read an account of Count Felix Von Luckner's World War I raids on allied commerce with *Seeadler,* a converted clipper ship that bore an uncanny resemblance to *Florida.* Von Luckner's exploits left a deep impression on the mind of the young reader and created a life-long interest in commerce raiders, an interest that eventually led to the writing of this book.

The Germans used a collection of ships as commerce raiders during both world wars. Some, such as *Emden,* were regular

warships but others, including the most successful, were converted merchant ships. For example, *Seeadler, Wolf,* and
Moewe used false flags and papers to trick the British into
allowing them to pass through the blockade as neutrals. During
World War II, the most successful German surface raider was
Atlantis, which often posed as a Dutch merchant ship and
ultimately sank twenty-two allied ships. Captains of these
raiders usually found uninhabited islands and out-of-the-way
locations to resupply their fuel bunkers after raiding their prizes
for food and other supplies. Two of the island depots often used
by Confederate raiders and later by the Germans were Fernando de Noronha and the Rocas, both in the South Atlantic.
The similarities between the operations of both the German
and the earlier Confederate raiders are so distinct that there can
be little doubt that the cruises of *Alabama* and *Florida* were
carefully studied by the commanders of these twentieth-century
surface raiders. The U boat or submarine may have been the
commerce raider of the future, but only a few U boats sank as
much tonnage as the more successful surface raiders.

Naval historians have seldom credited these commerce
raiders—and especially the surface raiders—with the success
which they deserve. Most naval history is written by former
naval officers, who are most often absorbed in fleet actions and
the great capital ships. Certainly naval tactics and the great
battles draw the most attention, being treated as infinitely
interesting subjects for study. Historians have frequently become so engrossed in these operations that they have lost sight
of the purpose of a navy.

The navy has always had two main functions. First, the
superior navy works to control the sea, and when it accom-
plishes this mission, it can then develop its second function,
projecting its power to any part of the world near the sea. The
country that controls the sea has access to all of the world's
resources and markets. Admiral Alfred T. Mahan in his classic
work *The Influence of Sea Power on History, 1660–1783* clearly
develops the theory that control of the sea was the basis of
world-wide British power and influence. If this power is to be
used, however, the nation must have an adequate merchant

fleet, without which no fleet of warships can reap any benefit from the sea.

The commerce raider is the weapon of a weaker naval power that has been driven from the open sea. Raiders hiding from warships are dispatched to capture or destroy the enemy's merchant fleet. In recent years this work has been largely entrusted to the submarine, whose function, like that of the raider, is to destroy the enemy's shipping. So far no country has won a war through commerce raiding, but the enemies have been damaged, sometimes greatly. In World War I and World War II the British would probably have been defeated had it not been for the intervention of the United States, with its large new fleet of merchant ships.

In the course of studying Confederate cruisers, it became apparent to this author that these ships did vast damage to the United States merchant service. While the Confederacy was not victorious, it was able to add a fatal push to a declining United States merchant marine. As explained in this study, the American merchant marine, even though suffering from subsidized competition by the British, was still operating successfully before the Civil War. It had not fallen to a level from which it could not have recovered. Had there been no war, there is a good chance the United States would have adopted a system of subsidies of its own with which to continue as a major competitor of the British.

In the first edition of this book, the account of shipping tonnage losses confused overseas shipping and coastal shipping. The American coastal trade was weakened by the raiders and by war risk insurance, but it largely survived the war. The major damage was to overseas shipping. In the 1850s the United States and Britain had a close rivalry in this business, but after war risk insurance and the commerce raiders finished their work, the best ships were in British hands and the attractive part of the overseas trade had been lost by the Americans. When the "queens of the sea" became too valuable to tie up and too expensive to insure, their owners either sold them or moved their registry overseas.

The United States merchant service has never recovered

from this loss. The Americans continued to ship coal and raw material, but the passenger trade was British-controlled after 1865. Other factors also figured in the decline, such as a diversion of capital to manufacturing and a turning away from the sea by many young men in America. Still, had the United States not lost so many of its finest ships, this trade would have very likely survived as more than a shadow of its former self.

The conclusions drawn two decades ago might benefit from a better distinction between overseas and coastal shipping, but the overall conclusions are as valid today as they were then. The cruisers were not able to win the war, but relative to their cost they did far more damage to the United States than any other class of military investment made by the Confederacy. In terms of damage to the long-range economy of the United States, the cruisers were more effective than any other single effort made by the Confederacy during the war.

October 1986   FRANK LAWRENCE OWSLEY, JR.

Preface

SOME HISTORIANS HAVE maintained that the Confederate cruisers had little, if any, effect on the outcome of the Civil War. Others have attributed a minor role to the cruisers. A detailed study of the C.S.S. *Florida* raises the question as to whether or not either of these is a valid conclusion. *Guerre de course,* or commerce raiding, is a naval application of guerilla warfare. It is just as much the weapon of a weak naval power as guerilla warfare is the weapon of a weak land force against a strong one. It is probable that commerce raiding has not been of great interest to military and naval historians in that it has done its greatest damage to the civilian economy rather than the military and naval forces of the nation against which it is conducted. This is a short-sighted view, and in a general study of the Civil War one can ill afford to neglect the recognized importance of Federal military operations against the Confederate economy. Commerce raiding was just as much a blow to the Federal economy, but since the United States was able to survive the losses, the significance of this weapon has often been overlooked. Actually, there is little reason to doubt that the losses to Union commerce and the coastal raids by the *Florida* and some of her sister ships added to a general war weariness in the North.

Considering the small number of cruisers and the relatively small investment involved, the commerce raiders more than paid for themselves in terms of direct damage to the war effort of the United States. This is clearly indicated by the fact that they sank more than 200 enemy merchant ships and diverted from other duties warships equaling more than ten times their own tonnage.

The indirect damage is far more impressive. Prior to the Civil War the United States merchant fleet was the second largest in the world, but by 1865 it was only a shadow of its former self, having been reduced by more than two-thirds. These important results from the point of view of the Confederacy were accomplished by a fleet of ships, some of which were built as cruisers while others were converted merchant ships, but all were capable of rendering enormous damage to the enemy.

A detailed study of the *Florida* illustrates, perhaps better than a study of any other cruiser, the full scale use by the United States of diplomatic warfare. Not only was the *Florida* subjected to all the diplomatic protests, harrassments, legal action and surveillance conducted against all the cruisers, but the capture of the ship in the neutral port of Bahia, Brazil, was instigated by the United States Minister to Brazil and the United States Consul at Bahia and with the full advance approval of Secretary of State William H. Seward. This unique incident alone shows clearly the importance the United States authorities placed upon the destruction of the cruisers.

Perhaps one reason why there has not been any serious attempt to study the entire career of the *Florida* in the past is because unlike the other major cruisers, the *Florida* had two commanders, and there was no single journal or memoir which covered her entire cruise. Since there is no one indi-

vidual around whom the account can be centered, this work
is the biography of the ship herself. This approach has the
advantage of permitting the story to be viewed through the
eyes of many different persons with various points of view,
a method which should give the reader a broader understand-
ing of the subject. In spite of the lack of a single memoir
from which to work, it is likely that there is more material
relating to the *Florida* available to the researcher than on
any other cruiser.

Although some of the log of the *Florida* was published in
summary form in the *Official Records of the Union and
Confederate Navies*, it was believed by the officials at the
National Archives, until a few years ago, that most of this
log had been lost. However, this author located the missing
volumes along with numerous other *Florida* papers and letter
books in the then unprocessed record group 76 which concerned the *Alabama* claims. It was therefore possible by
placing these records with the parts of the log which were
in the Navy records, record group 45, to reconstruct almost
the entire log of the *Florida*. This day by day account of
the ship has been invaluable to the study.

The *Official Records of the Union and Confederate Navies*
was, of course, a major source in this work. However, the
unpublished Navy records found in record group 45 in the
National Archives contain much material which has not been
published and has, therefore, been used very little prior to
this study. One part of these unpublished records, the
miscellaneous letters sent and miscellaneous letters received
by the Navy Department, were almost entirely overlooked
by the compilers of the *Official Records of the Union and
Confederate Navies*. These letters are most significant since
they are from private citizens and businesses and show
clearly the impact of the coastal raids of the *Florida* and her

"outfits." These records also reflect better than any other source the political and economic impact of cruiser warfare.

The Maffitt journal and Maffitt papers in the Southern Historical Collection at Chapel Hill were very useful for the first cruise of the ship and added much to the story. To round out the account and give a neutral point of view, a search of the British Public Record Office provided an excellent collection of *Florida* material.

The C.S.S. *Florida*

Chapter One

The Building of the *Florida*

STEPHEN R. MALLORY began his service as Confederate Secretary of the Navy in 1861 without ships and without the facilities with which to build them. Europe was the most likely source of an immediate supply of his needs, and he lost no time in sending his agents abroad with instructions to buy or build ships suitable for naval service. Of these agents, James D. Bulloch was by far the most capable. Formerly an officer in the United States Navy, he had returned to civilian life some years before the outbreak of the conflict. He was a man of ingenuity and fine judgment who understood the problems confronting Secretary Mallory. Bulloch's excellence was so well recognized that Lincoln's Secretary of State, William H. Seward, warned United States representatives abroad to be on the lookout especially for him and to keep him under close surveillance.[1]

Bulloch arrived in Liverpool, England, on June 4, 1861, and on the following day visited Charles K. Prioleau, resident agent of Fraser, Trenholm and Company in that town. This firm, partly owned in Charleston, South Carolina, was the principal commercial representative of the Confederacy in England. Bulloch learned from Prioleau that funds with which he was to buy or build ships had not yet arrived from the South, but because of the necessity for prompt action, Fraser, Trenholm and Company agreed to accept financial responsibility for any orders which Bulloch wished to make. With the financial backing of this firm, he was able almost immediately to make a contract for the *Florida,* first called the *Oreto,* and construction work on this ship was begun before the end of June, 1861.[2]

With the aid of Prioleau, Bulloch also made efforts to buy ships already constructed which would be suitable for naval use. He hoped to purchase large wooden steamers built for operation with either sail or steam which could cruise for long periods at sea. Such vessels would necessarily have to be built to carry large supplies of coal and also be well rigged for sailing. Equally important, the ships had to have a retractable screw, a feature seldom found in ordinary ships. A steamship that was to operate well under sail must be able to lift its screw out of the water for speed and ease of handling. Bulloch favored a strongly built wooden ship since the decks of iron ships built in that day were not considered strong enough to support the desired heavy guns. In addition to this, repairs to wooden ships could be made more easily in out-of-the-way ports lacking extensive ship building facilities.[3] However, because of the expense of timber in Britain, wooden ships were more costly than those constructed of iron.

Bulloch explained to Mallory the necessity for building ships capable of maintaining long cruising ranges. First of all, the blockade made it impossible for Confederate cruisers to depend on their own ports for supplies; secondly, because of the neutrality laws of various countries, cruisers would not be allowed to put into foreign ports for refueling and supplies more frequently than once every ninety days; and in the third place, the longer the ship could remain at sea, the more of the enemy's commerce she would destroy. Ships which met all these qualifications were not available, and it was soon obvious that it would be necessary to build rather than buy the kind of ships needed.

After investigating the various shipbuilding establishments, Bulloch selected the firm of William C. Miller and Sons of Liverpool to build the *Florida*. The senior member of that firm had been in the Royal Navy as a shipwright and had served Her Majesty's dockyards as a naval constructor. Miller was, therefore, experienced in building wooden ships designed to carry large crews and heavy loads of guns and equipment. Messrs. Fawcett, Preston and Company, also of Liverpool, were engaged to build the engines. In the beginning, Miller and Sons were the primary contractors and all financial arrangements were made through them; however, when the ship left the dockyard and was engaged in fitting out, most transactions were transferred to Fawcett and Preston, and nearly all later business which concerned repairs and replacement parts for the *Florida* was made with the latter firm.

Bulloch decided to use a dispatch gunboat of the Royal Navy as the basic model for the *Florida*. There were two good reasons for his choice. In the first place, this type of ship was fast and had most of the characteristics needed. Secondly, and perhaps more important, Miller and Sons had a scale drawing of such a ship, and it would save much time in construction to be able to use these plans with certain modifications. The length was increased to enable the ship to carry more coal and supplies and possibly to add to her speed. The rigging was also considerably increased over the original model for supplementary sailing facilities.

In order to keep secret the intended use of the ship, she was given the dockyard name of *Oreto*. This name had an Italian sound, and the people working on her in the dockyard were told that she was being built for a firm at Palermo, Italy.⁴ To add to this fiction, Bulloch was able to persuade John Henry Thomas, the local agent of the firm of Messrs. Thomas Brothers of Palermo, to supervise the construction of the vessel. The register of the *Oreto* indicated that she was the property of John Henry Thomas, a merchant of Liverpool.⁵ This deception was maintained even in her shipping orders. The crew was signed and the ship cleared port under orders showing her destination to be Palermo and the West Indies.⁶ According to the ship's register, she was not sold by Thomas to the Confederacy until February 5, 1863, in Nassau.⁷ Bulloch stated that he never told the builders the ship was destined for the Confederate government but made all arrangements in his own name. Undoubtedly, they knew the ultimate destination of the ship but no questions were asked.⁸ This had certain advantages in that the builders could honestly swear they had not been told the ship's intended use.

From the outset, Bulloch made every effort to keep out of trouble with the British government. He engaged F. S. Hull, a member of a leading firm of solicitors in Liverpool, to obtain an opinion from the best lawyers concerning the status of ships being built in Britain for the Confederacy. This was a difficult opinion to render since up to that time no ship had ever been seized under the provision of the Foreign Enlistment Act which prohibited the outfitting of warships in British Dominions for a belligerent power. Nevertheless, the opinion of the lawyers was that a ship could be legally built, regardless of the intended use of such a vessel, provided the ship was not equipped for war within British waters. This equipment was understood to mean guns and ammunition. Armed with these opinions, Bulloch made sure that none of the building contracts negotiated by him revealed the ultimate use or destination of the ships.' By carefully adhering to these provisions, he was able to prevent the condemnation of both the *Florida* and *Alabama*.

Bulloch did a thorough job of disguising his ships. Although construction on the *Oreto* was begun in June of 1861, the United States Minister to Britain, Charles Francis Adams, did not become suspicious of the vessel until the following October.[10] By November, even though Adams felt sure that construction of ships for the Confederacy was underway in Britain, he was not certain which vessels were involved.[11] It was not until late in January of 1862 that the investigators hired by United States officials were able to uncover any suspicious evidence on the *Oreto*. Even at this late date the ship was only suspected of being built for the South, and many facts concerning the construction were incorrect. Erroneous information obtained by United States' intelligence is revealed in the following dispatch from Thomas H. Dudley, United States Consul at Liverpool:

"The *Oritis* [*sic*] a screw gunboat is fitting out in one of the docks at this place, she is built of iron and is 700 tons. She is reported for the Italian Government, but the fact of the machinery being supplied by Fawcett and Preston and other circumstances connected with it made me suspicious, and causes me to believe she is intended for the South."[12]

Dudley continued his investigations, and by February 4, he had discovered that the Italian Consul knew nothing of the *Oreto* and did not think any warships were being built in Britain for his government.[13] A little later, Dudley was informed that the *Oreto* had taken two gun carriages on board. He now believed he had enough evidence to stop the vessel, and acting on this assumption, he sent his evidence to Adams, who could then enter a protest to the British government.[14] Adams took immediate action by sending Dudley's report to the British Foreign Secretary, Lord John Russell, along with a request that the British government investigate the suspicious vessel.[15] Shortly after this request was sent to Russell, Dudley's men discovered that Fawcett, Preston and Company had been paid to build the engines for the *Oreto* by Fraser, Trenholm and Company, known to be agents of the Confederacy. This information immediately dispelled any doubts which either Dudley or Adams may have had concerning the real owners of the *Oreto*.[16]

When presented with these facts, the British agreed to Adams' request and set about making an investigation of the *Oreto*. They first obtained a statement from W. C. Miller, an official of Miller and Sons, who gave a good description of the vessel and stated her owner to be Thomas Brothers of Palermo. Miller agreed that the *Oreto* had been built like a gunboat and believed Thomas Brothers intended to sell her to the Italian government.[17] In addition to the builder's statement, the British also obtained reports from their own customs officials who had examined the ship carefully. The customs authorities reported that they had been aware that the ship was built like a gunboat, and because of this fact, they had kept a very close watch on her activities. The report continued that they had been informed she was to be sold to the Italian government. The officials pointed out that regardless of who owned the vessel, she could not be seized because she had violated no law. She had no guns, gun carriages, or munitions of any kind on board, and, therefore, was a perfectly legal ship.[18] Although Russell continued the surveillance of the *Oreto* and the British government made further inquiries concerning her, the statements of the customs authorities and builder indicated that the ship was destined for Italy.[19]

At Liverpool, Consul Dudley continued his investigation, hoping to discover something which would cause the British government to seize the *Oreto*. He was reasonably certain by this time that the ship would leave port unarmed and would receive her war supplies after she left British waters. His investigations even uncovered the fact that the arms were supposed to be shipped on the *Bermuda*. This was a slight error since they were sent to Nassau on the *Bahama*. By the end of March, Dudley's observers had determined that the *Oreto* was ready for sea. He believed some of the Confederate naval officers who had recently arrived in Britain were there for the express purpose of taking her to sea.[20]

In the meantime, the British received a report from their minister to Italy indicating that that government knew nothing of the ship. The Italians reported that they were certain the *Oreto* was not intended for their navy.[21] Russell reported to Adams that he was now convinced the vessel was not bound for service with the Italian government, but he affirmed that his government had originally believed the *Oreto* to be an Italian ship. He told Adams that if it could be proved that this vessel was to be a warship, she would be seized and condemned. However, to be a warship she must have armament.[22] It is evident from this correspondence that Russell's view of what constituted a violation of the Foreign Enlistment Act was identical with the views of Bulloch's lawyers. Actually, the discovery of the nature of the *Oreto* came too late for Adams to conclude any action against her while she was still in Britain, although the later trial of the vessel at Nassau would indicate this made little difference.

On March 22, 1862, the *Oreto* quietly put to sea under the command of James A. Duguid, a British captain. Although she had already cleared the port authorities at the time of her sailing, most observers believed she was going on another trial trip. This false premise was based on the fact that there were several ladies and other visitors on board when she sailed. The ladies and part of the visitors were put ashore in small boats before she left the harbor, and the remainder, with one exception, left the ship in the pilot boat. The other passenger, a Mr. Low, put to sea with the ship. No one on board except the officers was aware that she was not bound for Palermo. The ship had been at sea for about ten days when the crew realized they should have reached Gibraltar if the destination were Palermo. Some thirty-seven days after leaving their anchorage in the River Mersey, the ship reached Nassau. Here, contrary to what they had expected, the crew was given no shore leave.[23] According to the statement of Thomas Gill, a crew member on the *Oreto,* the voyage to Nassau was not unusual except that the passenger, Mr. Low, seemed to have as much authority on board as the captain, and the ship ran without lights for the last four days before reaching port.[24] Low was Bulloch's agent with orders to deliver the ship.

Samuel Whiting, United States Consul at Nassau, reported the arrival of the *Oreto* on April 28, 1862, referring to her as another blockade runner.[25] It was not until the ship had been in port for two weeks that he addressed his first protest to the British authorities. He claimed that the *Oreto* was actually being armed in British waters and demanded that she be seized.[26] The British authorities answered Whiting's charge by saying that there were no arms on the ship, nor was there any proof that anyone planned to arm her. Whiting was reminded that if his charges were true, the owners of the *Oreto* were guilty of a misdemeanor, but positive evidence would be needed before any action could be taken.[27]

While the *Oreto* was at Nassau, she was not only the subject of much correspondence between the United States Consul and the British authorities, but there was also considerable discussion among the British officials themselves. Commander H. F. McKillop of HMS *Bulldog* reported that the *Oreto* was a very suspicious steamer which could be easily turned into a cruiser by putting some guns on board.[28] McKillop, after a few days' observation of the ship, became so positive that she was actually arming in the port that he seized her for violating the Foreign Enlistment Act. Governor C. J. Bayley and the rest of the civilian authorities at Nassau had not agreed to this action. Bayley pointed out that the *Oreto* was registered as a British ship, carried the British flag, and had no actual armament on board. Should she later change her nationality to one of the belligerents, she would then be a warship and would have to leave port within twenty-four hours. If she armed herself and cruised against commerce under the British flag, she would be seized as a pirate. The Governor emphasized the fact that if she tried to arm at Nassau, she would, of course, be seized under the Foreign Enlistment Act. Since the mysterious ship had done none of these things, he gave orders for her immediate release. He suggested, however, that McKillop keep the ship under close observation but urged him not to seize her again unless she were actually taking arms on board.[29] While the Governor could see no reason to seize the *Oreto,* he recognized the fact that she was a suspicious ship. He increased the surveillance by stationing customs officials at her anchorage, who examined everything that was taken on board to make sure no armament was loaded.[30] Nassau's Attorney General, G. L. Anderson, who was in agreement with

Bayley's views regarding the *Oreto,* stated that unless she had guns on board she was not legally a warship, and nothing would be gained by her seizure. An admiralty court would only set her free if she were not armed.[31] Although the *Oreto* had been released, the naval authorities were still not satisfied. Commander H. D. Hinckley of HMS *Greyhound,* McKillop's senior officer, arrived in port and assumed the duty of watching the suspicious vessel. He soon discovered that the *Oreto* was unloading shells and rightly suspected that she had actually been loading these shells until British officers were seen approaching the ship.[32] Hinckley's observations were correct according to the statement of Thomas Robertson, one of the *Oreto's* crew members. Captain Duguid, fearing the ship would again be seized, had ordered all shells removed when he observed boats from the *Greyhound* nearby.

Hinckley's discoveries created alarm among the Confederates, and on the following morning Duguid ordered the ship to sea, but the crew refused to raise the anchor. They stated that the articles under which they were serving had been broken when the ship went to Nassau instead of Palermo, and they refused to leave the port of Nassau until they knew their destination. Duguid told the men they were going to Havana for a cargo of coal, but this did not seem likely as the vessel's bunkers were already full of coal. The captain tried again and again to persuade the crew to take the ship to sea but to no avail. He then took them ashore, and the entire group went before a magistrate who agreed that the articles had been broken and that Duguid would have to pay all the men their wages through that day plus five pounds each for breaking the shipping articles. The crew demanded their passage money back to Britain in addition, but this request was refused, and they were ordered to remove their possessions and leave the ship. The disgruntled crew went ashore and immediately sought the advice of Commander Hinckley.[33] What these men told Hinckley is unknown, and whether vengeance was a motive is also unknown, but regardless of motives, they were successful in bringing about the second seizure of the *Oreto.*[34]

Governor Bayley was outraged by Hinckley's action and accused him of infringing on the rights of the civil authorities. Hinckley implied that he planned to take the case to a higher authority. Apparently, Hinckley did not believe proper action would be taken locally, and requested that the ship be sent to the vice admiralty court of either Bermuda or Halifax. Bayley considered this a personal insult and a slap at the competence of the civil officials at Nassau. He claimed that Hinckley had seized the ship on his own authority as senior naval officer in the colony and could expect no help from the civilian government.[35] Attorney General Anderson stated that as far as he could determine, Hinckley had no new evidence against the *Oreto,* and he still did not think the ship had violated the Foreign Enlistment Act.[34] Hinckley, under attack from all sides, agreed to release the vessel.

Governor Bayley was also under pressure; not only did his naval officers, Hinckley and McKillop, urge him to seize the vessel but the United States Consul wanted the ship tried before an admiralty court. In the face of this persistence, Bayley decided that a trial might be a good idea as it would quiet the various protests. Knowing the opinion of Anderson, Bayley was sure a trial of the *Oreto* before the admiralty court at Nassau would result in the ship's release. He, therefore, ordered the *Oreto* seized for the third time for violating the Foreign Enlistment Act, and to avoid delay, he added that she should be tried as soon as possible.[37]

The seizure and subsequent trial of the *Oreto* led to considerable joy among the United States officials. Perhaps in a spirit of thanksgiving, Consul Whiting wrote a letter to Hinckley expressing gratitude for his part in the seizure of the ship. Whiting naturally believed Hinckley was correct in his original action against the vessel and regretted that the civilian authorities at Nassau did not fully support him at that time.[38] In answering Whiting, Hinckley had the good judgment to deny that there was any difference of opinion concerning the seizure of the ship. He told Whiting that he was simply doing his duty and had the full cooperation of the civil authorities.[39] Governor Bayley was enraged by Whiting's action, which Bayley had interpreted as an insult to the civil authorities. The result was a request for Whiting's recall.[40] This did not lead to his immediate withdrawal, but it no doubt hindered the cause of the United States at Nassau.

The trial of the *Oreto* gave the United States' agents another chance at condemnation of the ship. Numerous sworn statements were produced by officials of the United States showing that the ship was a Confederate vessel.[41] The British government also obtained depositions from their various public officials who had had dealings with the *Oreto*. Copies of these statements indicating that the ship had not been armed were also given to Charles Francis Adams. The British hoped to prove to the United States once and for all that their government had not acted in bad faith.[42]

Whiting believed the evidence against the *Oreto* was overwhelming and that she would be condemned as a matter of course. When he learned Semmes and other Confederate officers had left Nassau for England, he was convinced that the Confederates themselves had given up hope.[43] However, before the trial ended, Whiting had changed his mind.[44] He had learned that Attorney General Anderson, who was directing the case against the vessel, was openly pro-Confederate and had made remarks in public to that effect. Although he had reported this to Anderson's superiors, Whiting doubted that it would aid his cause."

At the trial, testimony was heard from the *Oreto's* master and most of the other officers and crew members. Duguid and one or two officers testified that they knew of nothing irregular about the vessel and believed her to be an ordinary merchant ship. The crew's testimony and that of Commander Hinckley did not agree with the statement of Duguid. The crew and Hinckley claimed that she had shot lockers, magazines, and no cargo space. These men agreed that the *Oreto* was a perfect warship, lacking only guns which could easily be put on board in a matter of hours. While some of this testimony was challenged by the defense, it was at length determined that the *Oreto* was designed like a warship, but she was not legally a warship since she had no guns on board. This fact alone satisfied the judge that the vessel had not violated the Foreign Enlistment Act, and she was released."

Needless to say, Consul Whiting was not satisfied with the conduct of this trial, and he was disappointed in the outcome. He reported that Judge Lees had accepted the word of hired sailors over that of Commander Hinckley, an officer in the Royal Navy. Whiting also believed the log book of the *Oreto* should have been given more consideration at the trial; it could certainly have proved the true character of the vessel. He complained that the court did not once raise the question of the ship's ultimate destination and use."

An examination of the correspondence of Governor Bayley and the other officials at Nassau leaves little doubt that these men were pro-Confederate. They did their jobs within the law, but as the United States Consul observed, their sympathies were Confederate. This pro-southern sentiment was later observed by Commander J. N. Maffitt when he put into port on board the *Florida* in January, 1863. Maffitt interviewed Governor Bayley at that time and came away with the distinct impression that he was pro-Confederate. Maffitt also commented on the fact that all the citizens of Nassau were most amiable and helpful.[48]

Even though the officials at Nassau leaned to the South and doubtless intended to release the *Oreto* from the beginning, it should be noted that the ship did not violate the understood meaning of the Foreign Enlistment Act, and in the legal opinion given to Bulloch, no ship disobeyed the law unless it was armed. An armed vessel according to definition was a ship not only designed to carry guns but one actually having guns on board. This was true no matter what else could be proved about the ship. While a less friendly court might have delayed the *Oreto* for a longer period of time, the issue was the same as that of the *Alexandra*, which was ultimately released by the high courts of Britain.[49] It can, therefore, be assumed that the case of the *Oreto* would have come to the same conclusion whether it was tried in Britain or in Nassau.

When Whiting learned that the *Oreto* was to be released, he called for support from the United States Navy, requesting ships to be sent to intercept the vessel as she left port.[50] The Navy followed the Consul's advice, and within a few days there were United States warships in the Nassau area.[51]

These various difficulties encountered by the *Oreto* could have been avoided had she not remained in port for such an extended period. The real reason this ship was not taken out of port more quickly can be traced directly to the great confusion over who was to command her. Low, Bulloch's representative, had been ordered by Bulloch to find Lieutenant J. N. Maffitt at Nassau and turn over command of the ship immediately. Unfortunately, Maffitt, who was engaged in blockade running, was not in port when Low arrived. Low was, therefore, forced to wait two weeks until Maffitt returned.[52]

Upon receiving these orders, Maffitt gave up the blockade runner *Nassau* and assumed responsibility for the *Oreto*. This, however, was only the beginning of the confusion. Not only was Maffitt without officers and crew for the new ship, but he also needed to have Bulloch's orders confirmed by Secretary Mallory and to receive cruising orders. Therefore, Maffitt immediately wrote Mallory requesting orders and a crew. In the meantime, he had to wait, not daring to go near the *Oreto* lest it be positively identified as a warship. In due course, he received his reply from Mallory which stated that the *Oreto* was to be given to Commander J. S. North, who would arrive in Nassau on the British steamer *Bahama*, which was also carrying the armament. The Secretary approved Maffitt's conduct in taking responsibility for the ship, but he was apparently unaware that North had refused command of the vessel. Mallory did, however, order Maffitt to retain responsibility, and in case North did not arrive on the *Bahama*, he was to consider himself in command. The Secretary also detailed Passed Master O. Bradford and Acting Midshipman Sinclair to serve as officers on the *Oreto*, leaving Maffitt to recruit a crew and giving him authority to commission enough officers to man the ship. Maffitt was extremely unhappy over this situation since he considered Bradford incompetent and had no idea where he was going to obtain officers and crew on such short notice.

Maffitt realized that the delay of the ship was exceedingly dangerous because every day the United States representatives were demanding her seizure and supplying more evidence for British authorities. Nevertheless, he had to await the *Bahama*, which, of course, arrived without North. Since the *Oreto* was seized the following day, Maffitt had no opportunity to take command of the ship.[53] When he, at length, did assume command, surveillance was such that it was impossible either to load arms and equipment or to recruit a crew in Nassau. Eventually the guns and munitions were loaded on the schooner *Prince Albert* and shipped to an uninhabited island nearby to await the *Oreto*. Once the ship had been released by the British, Maffitt left immediately with all the officers and men he could muster to meet the *Prince Albert*.[54]

Maffitt had learned that there were several Union warships in the Nassau area and more were expected. Since the United States steamer *R. R. Culyer* was already in the harbor observing the movements of the *Oreto*, he got his ship to sea as quickly as possible. On August 8, the day after her release, the *Oreto* got underway, but as soon as she was noted to be leaving port, the *Culyer* followed her. Maffitt realized almost at once that the other ship was in pursuit, and, as a countermeasure, he brought his ship to anchor in the entrance of the harbor next to the British warship *Petrel*. The *Culyer* circled the *Oreto* several times, whereupon the *Petrel's* captain ordered the Union vessel either to return to the harbor or get out of British territorial waters, and the *Culyer* put to sea. This action of the *Petrel*, which was commanded by a Captain Watson, a good friend of Maffitt, probably saved the Confederate ship from capture. As soon as the *Culyer* was well out, Maffitt got his ship under way once more and set a course which appeared to be toward Charleston. The *Culyer*, observing this action from a distance, also set a course for Charleston under full steam.

In the meantime, Maffitt, still close to land, had sailed his ship into the shadow of Hog Island where he once more came to anchor.[55] As soon as the *Culyer* was out of sight, he raised the anchor and sailed westward, remaining close to the coast and in the shadow of the islands. When the ship reached the west end of the island, he changed course to due south and met the *Prince Albert*. The *Oreto* took the *Prince Albert* in tow and reached Green Cay, an uninhabited island, at about 3:00 p.m. on August 9. As soon as the ships anchored, work commenced transferring the armament. Since the ship had such a small crew, it was necessary for the officers and men alike to work at getting the guns and munitions on board. Even with the officers assisting, there were so few hands that the guns and munitions were not fully loaded on board until August 16.[56] On the 17th, with the guns mounted and apparently ready for action, the *Oreto* was officially christened the *Florida* and commissioned into the Confederate Navy.[57]

Chapter Two

The *Florida* at Mobile

THE "FLORIDA" AS A warship was not unusually powerful. There were many ships of her general class in the United States Navy. She was slightly smaller than her sister ship the *Alabama*, having a displacement of 700 tons as compared with the *Alabama's* 1,050. She had a rated top speed under steam and sail of twelve knots, although she bettered this during her first cruise, making fourteen and one half knots during her run from Mobile in January, 1863. This made the *Florida* a fast ship for her day, but the United States had a number of ships that boasted of a greater speed. The *Florida's* armament consisted of two seven-inch Blakely rifles mounted on pivot and six six-inch Blakely rifles.¹ There have been some conflicting reports regarding her armament, with some naval observers stating that she had six smooth bore 32 pounders in broadside, rather than Blakely rifles. This discrepancy probably resulted from the fact that the six-inch guns were smooth bore 32 pounders of an older pattern that had been converted to rifles, probably at the Blakely foundry. She was bark-rigged and her hull was

designed like the famous clipper ship, doubtless accounting
for her good speed. She was a beautiful vessel.[2]

The first captain of the *Florida*, Lieutenant John Newland
Maffitt of North Carolina, was a man well suited to the task
of commanding a commerce raider. The son of an Irish
Methodist minister, he had been born at sea while his parents
were immigrating. He was forty-two years old at the outbreak
of the Civil War and had been in the United States Navy
since 1832, having entered as a midshipman at the age of
thirteen. Maffitt had in his twenty-nine years in the navy
served on almost every type of ship. His long tour with the
coast survey had given him an intimate knowledge of the
shore line of the United States and was one of the reasons
he was chosen early in the war to command a Confederate
blockade runner. He returned to blockade running after end-
ing his command on the *Florida,* and his success in this
capacity rivaled his reputation as captain of the *Florida.*
Maffitt had the audacity and imagination needed to command
a successful blockade runner and was also an ideal captain
of a commerce raider where boldness and ingenuity were
equally important.[3] It seems probable that had Maffitt been
able to command the *Florida* during her entire career, she
would have been a better known ship even than the
Alabama.

The difficulties encountered while getting the *Florida*
armed and out of Nassau were only the beginning of her
problems. In the first place, although the *Florida* had guns
and ammunition on board, it was soon discovered that the
rammers, sponges, sights and other essential items of equipment had been left behind in the haste and confusion of loading the *Prince Albert.* Thus, the fine armament was completely useless. In the second place, the ship had a crew of
only thirteen men and fourteen officers, most of whom

lacked sea experience. This force was further reduced with the advent of six cases of yellow fever on board.' With a crew as small as this, it would not have been feasible to operate the guns even if their equipment had been complete. The force was so reduced that it could not operate the ship efficiently. Since it was utterly impossible to begin the cruise at this time, Maffitt ran the ship into Cardenas, Cuba. The *Florida* was well received by the Spanish authorities who gave the officers and crew much needed medical aid. By this time a large part of the ship's complement, including Maffitt, had fallen victim to yellow fever. Because of the inadequate medical care on board ship, the Spanish removed the sick and sent them to hospitals ashore.' Six died, including Maffitt's step-son, Acting Paymaster I. L. Read, and not more than three or four of the remaining crewmen were physically able to perform their duties. Fortunately, twelve new recruits were signed on at Cardenas, but even with these additions the ship was dangerously undermanned. Dr. R. H. Barrett, a surgeon from Georgia, realizing the need of his services on board the Confederate ship, resigned his position with the Spanish government and joined the crew of the *Florida* with the rank of Acting Assistant Surgeon.'

In the meanwhile, the United States authorities had discovered the *Florida's* location and had posted several warships outside Cardenas. There were rumors that these ships planned to cut the cruiser out of the harbor, which offered little or no protection. Because Cardenas was already under surveillance, the *Florida* awaited an opportunity to make a run to Havana. The opportunity was provided on August 31, 1862, when at 8:00 in the evening, a Spanish mail steamer left Cardenas bound for Havana. The United States ships, mistaking the mail steamer for the *Florida,* chased her down the coast and fired on her. Once the Federal ships were well away in pursuit of the wrong quarry, the *Florida* put to sea and arrived at Havana at 11 : 30 the next morning.

Upon reaching his destination, Maffitt soon discovered that there were no seamen available to add to the crew of his ship. The prevalence of yellow fever at this time of the year caused seamen to avoid the city. The Spanish authorities also refused to allow the *Florida* to take on board any equipment which could be used to make her guns serviceable. Thus handicapped with insufficient crewmen and no usable armament, Maffitt decided to run the ship into a Confederate port. He learned while at Havana that there were only a few ships blockading the port of Mobile, and being fairly familiar with this area he decided to run the *Florida* into that port.

Realizing that Federal cruisers were already gathering outside the port of Havana, Maffitt determined to put to sea immediately. At 9:00 p.m. on September 1, the *Florida* sailed from Havana. In order to elude the enemy, Maffitt kept his ship close to the coast for some distance and headed toward the open sea only after he was reasonably sure he had avoided pursuit.[7] The voyage to Mobile was conducted without incident. One United States steamer was sighted but proved to be entirely too slow to overtake the Confederate ship.[8]

At 3:00 in the afternoon on September 4, Maffitt sighted Fort Morgan at Mobile Bay. Information regarding the strength of the blockade at this place had been correct. There were in sight only two steamers, the *Oneida* and the *Winona*. Lieutenant J. M. Stribling, the *Florida's* executive officer, was of the opinion that no attempt should be made to enter the harbor until after dark because of the crippled condition of the ship and her inability to offer any resistance. Maffitt rejected this plan for several reasons. The lighthouse had been eliminated, and the Confederates had removed the buoys which marked the channel. Since he lacked these aids and since he was aware of the *Florida's* deep draft, he thought it would be impossible for the ship to get into Mobile Bay at night without a pilot.

At the same time Maffitt realized that, if he chose daylight, it would be necessary to pass very near one or both of the blockading ships; without usable guns there would be little chance for the *Florida* to remain afloat. Taking all of these things into consideration in the manner of an expert poker player, he concluded that the only way to get his ship through the blockading squadron was by surprise and sheer bluff. The *Florida* was built exactly like a British warship, and it was not unusual for Her Majesty's vessels to approach the blockade and ask for permission to proceed. Maffitt chose this disguise for the Confederate cruiser. He did not expect to be able to pass all the way through the blockade undetected, but he did hope the ruse might get him part of the way. He was, in fact, capitalizing on the recent difficulties the United States had had with Britain over the *Trent* affair. He believed that this would cause a Union commander to deliberate very carefully before firing on a British ship Raising the British flag, Maffitt steamed directly toward the *Oneida,* flagship of the squadron, as if to request permission to pass through the blockade.

The *Oneida* held her fire and steered to cut off the *Florida.* Maffitt did not change his course, and George H. Preble. commander of the *Oneida,* fearing a collision, backed his ship. This gave Maffitt the momentary advantage he needed because Preble allowed the *Florida* to come within eighty yards before he fired the first warning shot across her bow. The Confederate ship did not waver in her course, and Preble fired a second warning shot which was quickly followed by a broadside. At this close range, the *Oneida* could easily have sunk the ship but her guns were not fully depressed and the only result of the broadside was to carry away some of the *Florida's* rigging. This error lost Preble his golden opportunity to blast the *Florida* out of the water. At this time, a third Federal ship, a sailing vessel, appeared on the scene, giving the cruiser three enemy ships to elude.

When Preble commenced his action against the Confederate ship, the other two blockaders simultaneously opened fire, but their shots were also high. Maffitt had ordered the British flag hauled down and the Confederate flag raised in its place at the first firing from the *Oneida.* According to the log of the *Florida,* the British ensign was lowered, but the broken rigging of the ship prevented the Confederate colors from being immediately raised.

Having missed the *Florida's* vital parts with their first broadsides, the Federal ships concentrated their fire on her hull. The second barrage was far more effective than the first. One eleven inch shell from the *Oneida* passed through the coal bunkers on the port side near the water line, grazed the forward boilers, killed fireman James Duncan, and wounded several other men. Had this shell exploded, it would probably have sunk the *Florida* or wrecked at least one of her boilers. Still another shell passed through the cabin and the pantry, and another one exploded close to the port gangway, causing some serious damage to the ship. Soon after the firing started, Maffitt attempted to set the sails, but the Federal ships fired shrapnel into the rigging, and only a small amount of sail could be set. When it became apparent to Maffitt that the ship's sails would be useless, he ordered all men below except the two at the wheel, and the ship steamed full speed ahead.

The *Florida* survived this clash with the blockading squadron largely because of Maffitt's effective strategy. He had avoided all fire from the United States ships until he had actually passed them. The rattled gun crews of the Federal ships failed to inflict serious damage with their first broadsides fired at extremely close range. After reloading, the second broadsides were more effective but failed again to hit the vitals of the Confederate ship. The third round was fired into the *Florida*'s rigging, preventing the use of her sails. These last shots succeeded in their purpose but failed to do any serious damage to the ship. The *Florida* was faster than either the *Oneida* or the *Winona,* and with each round of fire she increased the distance between herself and her pursuers. She had already passed the blockading ships when the action started, and the Federal ships were forced to pursue her. Maffitt succeeded in maneuvering the enemy blockaders into a line, so that only the leading ship, the *Oneida,* could fire. The *Winona* could not fire after the first broadside for fear of hitting the *Oneida.*⁹ Once the *Florida* was ahead of the Federal ships, the *Oneida* had to yaw out of line in order to bring her broadside guns to bear on the cruiser, and after firing, turn back into line, and continue the pursuit. The maneuvers took time, and the distance between the *Florida* and her pursuers increased rapidly with each successive broadside.¹⁰ Eventually, the *Florida* drew out of range and at dusk was safely under the guns of Fort Morgan.¹¹

Commander Preble's account of the action more than any of the others demonstrated the effectiveness of Maffitt's ruse and evasive action. Preble reported that the mysterious ship had every appearance of an English man-of-war. As soon as he saw her approaching, he signaled the *Winona* to chase her and the two steamers advanced toward the stranger. Preble's official report stated that even at the close distance of one hundred yards, the Florida appeared to be an

English warship, and so he ordered a shot to be fired across her bow. When the stranger failed to heed the warning shot, he fired another before he gave a broadside. Preble and his gun crews were confused by the strange action of what appeared to be an English vessel; this fact was undoubtedly responsible for the poor aim of the first broadside. Although Maffitt made no mention of it in the log, Preble claimed that after the *Oneida's* broadside the *Florida* turned her pivot guns toward the United States ship. It may be that an expectation of a broadside from the *Florida* slowed the activity of the *Oneida's* gun crews or perhaps made them nervous, spoiling their aim on the second broadside. Preble credited the *Florida's* ultimate escape to her great speed which enabled her to get out of range quickly.[11] The entire action lasted only twenty-four minutes; the first shots were fired at 6:03, and the last at 6:27 p.m. Not only did darkness break the action but the *Oneida* very nearly grounded, running into shallow water close to the guns of Fort Morgan.[12]

Not everyone aboard the *Oneida* agreed with Preble's account of the action. H. W. Wilson, who kept a diary while serving on the ship, described the battle with the *Florida* in a light which was far less favorable to Preble. He complained bitterly that Preble showed great reluctance to open fire on the *Florida* and actually gave three warning shots rather than two before loosing a broadside. The third shot, which passed between the fore and main mast of the Confederate ship, may have been mistaken by Maffitt as a shot fired in anger. Wilson was convinced that the *Oneida* could have easily sunk the *Florida* had she begun the action soon enough, but thanks to Preble's delay, the cruiser was nearly out of range when the Federal ship began firing in earnest. Wilson agreed that the *Florida's* superior speed saved her, and that a heavy swell struck the *Oneida* just as she fired her first broadside, causing her shells to pass over the Confederate, but he was certain that the prize was lost by Preble's indecision.[14] Preble's reasons for his failure were legion. In addition to the *Florida's* speed, he complained bitterly that he had not been warned of the possible presence of the Confederate ship. This alone had made him prone to accept without suspicion the approach of a "British warship." Preble also explained that the *Florida's* speed was doubly effective since the *Oneida* could get steam from only one boiler; the other was being repaired. As a result of his failure to capture or sink the *Florida,* Preble was dismissed from the United States Navy. He was later reinstated but only after considerable pressure had been brought on the Navy Department by his friends.[15]

It is ironic that Preble, whose naval career was nearly ruined by this action, was one of Maffitt's oldest friends. The two had been close friends since they had served together as midshipmen on the U.S.S. *Constitution* in 1835, and their friendship was resumed after the war when they corresponded regularly until Preble's death in 1885. Although he was restored to duty, Preble was not restored to his proper rank until a special court of inquiry was held in May of 1872, at which time Maffitt's testimony was influential in clearing him of negligence.[16]

The first order of business for the *Florida* after reaching Mobile Bay was to bury her dead and make some effort to clear the wreckage of the recent action. The damage to the ship, though it was extensive, did not endanger her. The rigging had borne the brunt of the Federal fire.[17] Since there were still cases of yellow fever on board, and since Lieutenant Stribling contracted the disease shortly after the ship's arrival, the *Florida* was placed in quarantine.[18] Stribling died on September 12. In spite of the quarantine, Admiral Franklin Buchanan visited Maffitt on September 8 and praised the officers and crew for their action. The *Florida* remained in isolation until September 30, during which time there was little done to the ship beyond keeping her clean, since about half the men of the already small crew were on the sick list.[19] The only person who reported for duty was Assistant Surgeon F. Garretson, a needed replacement for Dr. Barrett, whose health was too poor for him to continue his service. Garretson had formerly served in the United States Navy under the name of Van Biber, but he changed his name to Garretson upon entering the Confederate Navy to avoid reprisals against his family who lived in Maryland, an area controlled by the United States.[20]

Repairs on the *Florida* were not begun until October 3, after the quarantine had been lifted. The shortage of skilled workers and ordnance supplies made this a slow and tedious task, and the guns were not completely equipped until the early part of January, 1863.[21] Maffitt blamed this long delay on several factors. First of all, the *Florida,* because of her draft, had to remain twenty-eight miles south of Mobile. This meant all workers had to be brought from the city by boat, and any of the *Florida's* equipment requiring mechanical facilities for repair had to be dismantled, taken to the city, brought back, and re-installed. The ship was anchored in the open bay, and rough winter weather often stopped work completely. The worst damage to the ship had been done to the wire standing rigging which had to be spliced or replaced, a slow tedious job any time, and impossible in bad weather.[22] Maffitt's journal reflects the fact that he and his men became restless with the long delay in leaving port.

The difficulties involved in getting repairs made and obtaining necessary military supplies are indicative of the tremendous problems faced by the Confederacy in the con-

duct of the war. At least six weeks of the delay appears to
have been a direct result of shortages. While it is unquestion-
ably true that the presence of the *Florida* in Mobile did, as
Admiral Buchanan believed, force the Union to employ a
large number of ships in watching for the cruiser, there is
little doubt that Maffitt could have made many more captures
had he been able to put to sea sooner."

The *Florida's* prolonged delay in leaving Mobile not only
stirred discontent aboard the ship, but it also caused no small
amount of unrest in Richmond. Secretary Mallory, apparently believing the delay was caused by Maffitt's unwilling-
ness to leave the safety of Mobile, relieved him from duty
and ordered Lieutenant Joseph N. Barney to take command.
What precipitated Mallory's sudden decision is a mystery
and cannot be documented. Upon receiving this order,
Maffitt immediately conferred with Admiral Buchanan, who
had not been consulted regarding the action. Buchanan was
very much disturbed by Maffitt's removal." The Admiral
wrote Mallory a rather detailed letter in which he explained
that the ship had taken considerable time and effort to repair
and that there had been a general lack of inclement weather
which would be necessary to run her past the eight or nine
blockading ships. Buchanan continued to explain that in no
way was Maffitt at fault and was due praise rather than
rebuke. It is apparent from the tone of this letter that
Buchanan felt the Secretary had been undermining his authority, and he was insulted." In addition to his letter to
Mallory, Buchanan immediately visited President Davis who
happened to be in Mobile, and persuaded him that Maffitt
had been done a great injustice. Davis must have agreed
with the Admiral since he telegraphed Mallory and Maffitt
was restored to the *Florida*.

In his journal Maffitt expressed his opinion of Mallory's

action as follows: "Mr. Mallory, with characteristic little-
ness of mind, has permitted surreptitious naval gossip to
operate, with the least magnanimity of soul or manliness of
purpose."[26] His journal contains many references to Mallory
which indicate that he disagreed with the Secretary's conduct
of his office. He believed that Mallory was not suited for the
job of Secretary of the Navy, both because of his failure to
understand the needs of the Confederacy, and because of
his favoritism for a small group of friends, many of whom
Maffitt thought to be incompetent. Although he never said
so, Maffitt implied that Commander Barney, his relief, was
one of this group. He had been especially critical of the
Secretary's preparations of the defense of Port Royal, which
he, Maffitt, believed could have been held had a proper
defense been established. The real reason for Maffitt's dis-
like of Mallory doubtless dated back to the period of
Maffitt's service in the United States Navy. Mallory, as chair-
man of the Naval Affairs Committee of the Senate during
the 1850's, was responsible for the "infamous" Naval Retir-
ing Board which retired many well known officers including
Maffitt. However, Maffitt was restored after a hearing.[27]

Apparently the delay of the *Florida* at Mobile did cause
widespread interest and considerable criticism. An account
of Maffitt's removal in the *London Times* indicated that
Mallory had relieved Maffitt because of this harsh criticism.
The article further explained that President Davis had
restored him upon learning the true circumstances.[28]

While in Mobile, the *Florida* at last received a crew and
full complement of officers. Concerning the new men, Maffitt
wrote in his journal that many of the crew "rated as seamen
who in the old service would merely pass as very ordinary
O.S. [Ordinary Seamen]." Because many of the new men
were from the merchant service and were not well trained in

duties on a warship, Maffitt was undoubtedly able to use the
time spent at Mobile to some advantage in training his crew
and establishing discipline.[29] It should be noted that because
the *Florida* had put into the port of Mobile, some of the
crew for the cruise were actually Southerners, having families
in the Confederacy, and even though the majority was
foreign born, they were at least recruited openly for the
Confederate Navy.[30]

As to the officers, Maffitt complained that the personnel
had to be changed several times while the ship was in port.
In fact, so fluid were the officer billets that he did not know
who his officers would be until he was ready to put to sea.
However, he indicated that he was very well pleased to be
rid of some of those who had been assigned to him. He
managed to transfer two who had come on board at Nassau
whom he believed to be unfit. These were Acting Master O.
Bradford, whom Maffitt described as a malcontent of little
ability, and A. Vesterling, Paymaster's Clerk, whom he considered a "pest" and a "jackass." He also arranged for the
transfer of the ship's executive officer, Lieutenant Dulany A.
Forrest, characterized as a "most unfortunate selection, but
'tis not his fault that heaven has not formed him with
brains." His only criticism of the final selections was that
they were a very young group, but at the same time he
believed they would mature into fine officers. Maffitt, pleased
with the appointments of Lieutenants J. S. Hoole and S. W.
Averett, was especially happy to get Lieutenant C. W. Read,
who was assigned to the ship at the captain's own request.
Read had a reputation for being a bit slow witted, but had,
nevertheless, acquired an excellent combat record in the
defense of New Orleans.[31] Maffitt's faith in Read was well
founded for he was destined to become one of the most
outstanding young naval officers in the Confederacy.

Secretary Mallory's instructions to Maffitt for the up-coming cruise were of a general nature, leaving the area in which the ship would sail entirely to the captain's discretion. Mallory suggested that it would be a vital blow to the enemy if the *Florida* were to capture one or two of the treasure ships bringing gold from California. Such a feat would not only be very useful to the Confederacy but would also impair the Union's finances and credit. The Secretary thought it would be necessary to destroy most prizes because it would be very difficult to run the blockade with such a captured ship. He also cautioned Maffitt that even though the United States was making extensive use of the British flag to protect cargoes, the *Florida* was dependent on foreign ports and could not afford to offend neutrality. Maffitt was further instructed to obtain pilots for the Bahamas and the West Indies since he would no doubt wish to operate in that area. He was also given the authority to act as an agent of the Confederacy when the need arose. As for communication, Maffitt was to obtain two small English dictionaries, one to be retained on board his ship, and the other to be sent to the Navy Department. The code was to be the number of the page and the number of the word on the page, counting from the top.[32]

Maffitt also received orders from Admiral Buchanan to the effect that the *Florida* should be painted lead color when she ran the blockade, since this color would be extremely difficult to observe at night. Buchanan also instructed him to be ready for an engagement when passing through the block-ade, while at the same time avoiding action if possible.[33]

The *Florida*, though ready for sea by January 10, 1863, was forced to wait for a dark night to escape. While being maneuvered around Mobile Bay, the ship ran aground, and the crew spent the next two days trying to refloat her, a task which finally necessitated unloading the guns and coal before the steamers *Morgan* and *Gaines* were able to tow her free.[34] The hard-luck ship then ran aground again before sailing out of the bay and a second time had to be unloaded.[35] By January 16, the ship was once more ready to leave port, and although she needed bad weather to pass the blockade, the pilot considered it too unfavorable to get out. The visibility at that time was such as to make it impossible to navigate the ship. However, at 2:00 a.m. on January 17, the rain ceased and while there was still a great mist, the *Florida* at last got underway.

On the way out of Mobile Bay, she was forced to pass close to three blockading ships. She managed to pass the first two undetected but was discovered by the third. As soon as Maffitt realized he had been sighted, he ordered full steam and all sails to be set, enabling the ship to outrun her pursuers quickly. Later that morning the cruiser passed close to a very large warship believed to be the *Brooklyn*. Fortunately for the *Florida*, the Federal ship mistook the cruiser for another United States vessel and passed on by paying no attention to her.[36] The rest of the day elapsed without incident until about five in the afternoon when the Confederates sighted two more ships, one of which was the *R. R. Culyer*. Maffitt feared the *Culyer* more than any ship in the blockade because she was rated as a faster ship than the *Florida* and had been sent to Mobile especially to catch the cruiser. Realizing the *Culyer's* speed, he determined to try to escape observation by the Federal ship. Since it was rapidly growing dark and the *Culyer* was about three miles away, he ordered all sail taken in and shut down the ship's engines. The sea was somewhat rough, and the high swells would tend to hide the low lying hull of the Confederate vessel. Maffitt had again calculated correctly, and the *Culyer* passed by without seeing the *Florida*. Once Maffitt was satisfied the lookouts on the enemy ship had not seen him, he set sail again and steamed to the south. On this run the *Florida* made a record fourteen and one-half knots, the best of her entire career. No more ships were sighted on that day, and by the next morning she was well away from the coast.[37]

Commander George F. Emmons of the *Culyer* later reported he had chased the *Florida* for most of the day before losing sight of her in the late afternoon. He had, however, probably been chasing the *Florida's* smoke, since his ship was not seen by the cruiser until near sunset. The *Culyer* had failed to reach her target because she had several leaks in her boilers and could not keep up full steam.[38] When Emmons lost sight of the ship, he proceeded in the direction of the Yucatan, which he believed to be the *Florida's* destination. He had been informed by a captured pilot from Mobile that the Confederate ship had left there with three hundred men on board. Since this would be far more than she would need for a regular crew, he assumed she was carrying a crew for another ship. A large and suspicious steamer had been seen near the coast of the Yucatan, and Emmons set a course for that point.[39]

Once free of the *Culyer*, Maffitt considered the *Florida* to be out of danger and began his first cruise not toward the Yucatan but against the commerce of the United States.[40]

Chapter Three

First Cruise

IMMEDIATELY AFTER ESCAPING from Mobile, the *Florida* began her first cruise. The ease with which the ship had eluded the blockading squadron was a credit to her twenty officers and 116 men.[1] They were an odd mixture of old navy men, former merchant men and raw recruits. For two days the *Florida* steered southward without encountering a single ship.

On the third day, January 19, 1863, the brig *Estelle* of New York, bound from Santa Cruz, Cuba, to Boston with a cargo of honey and sugar, was sighted and captured.[2] The prize crew burned the ship after removing the personnel and their baggage. According to Captain John Brown, the ship was on her maiden voyage and was worth over $130,000. He thought his ship should have been spared since the cargo was Spanish property consigned by Venecia Roderguez and Company to an American firm. Aside from the disagreeable nature of their confinement, Brown reported that his men were well treated during their two day stay on board the *Florida*.[3]

After steaming at full speed for several days to avoid pursuit, the coal bunkers of the *Florida* had become depleted, and Maffitt decided to take his ship to Havana for refueling. The *Florida* carried only enough coal for nine days of full steaming. He also needed to buy clothing for the crew, whom he described as being nearly nude, a situation which attested to the shortage of clothing in the Confederacy. At the entrance to Havana harbor the *Florida* was hailed by the guard boat, but failing to understand the signal, Maffitt ran his ship into the harbor and anchored. As it was still early evening, he went ashore and called upon Major Charles Helm, the Confederate agent at this post. The next morning Maffitt discovered that he had violated a new port regulation by entering Havana at night without permission. Since he was not aware of the new rule, his apology to the authorities was accepted without difficulty. He requested and was granted permission to obtain coal and provisions for his ship. He noted in his journal that the people of Havana expressed marked pro-Southern feelings.[4]

As was to be expected, R. W. Shufeldt, the United States Consul General at Havana, protested violently to the Spanish authorities for allowing the *Florida* to obtain coal and provisions. Shufeldt stated that the ship had just destroyed a Spanish owned cargo, the *Estelle,* and should not have been allowed to enter Havana. He wanted the Confederate ship delayed for at least twenty-four hours since an American ship had just left port. The *Florida* was not detained and apparently the Spanish officials paid little attention to the protests of the Consul. It is interesting to note that while Shufeldt was demanding the detention of the *Florida,* he was also trying to communicate the location of the Confederate vessel to one of the United States cruisers in the area.[5]

Realizing that Federal warships would soon arrive, Maffitt put to sea at daybreak on January 22, and shortly after leaving port captured the brig *Windward* of New York. The *Windward* was seized four miles from the Cuban port of Matanzas, which she had just left.⁶ The ship's captain, Richard Roberts, stated later that the Confederate ship was flying the British flag when she stopped him, and the Rebel flag was not raised until after his ship had been captured. The officers and crew of the prize were given their choice of going on board the *Florida* or taking to the small boats. They were close to land and chose to row ashore. The prize was then stripped of valuables and burned.⁷

Later in the day, the *Florida* captured the brig *Corris Ann* of Machias, Maine, with a cargo of barrel staves. Captain Fredrick H. Small of the *Corris Ann* reported that he was waiting for a pilot boat just outside the port of Cardenas at the time of his capture. Small said his ship was near Stone Cay, and he believed they were in Spanish waters. He also protested that the *Florida* flew the British flag until the prize crew started coming on board his ship.⁸

Shortly after leaving port, Maffitt discovered that the coal which he had obtained at Havana was worthless and could make only enough steam for about three knots.⁹ Since there were Federal warships in the area, it was necessary to throw some of the inferior coal overboard so the remainder of the good fuel obtained at Mobile could be reached. This again caused a shortage of coal and forced Maffitt to take the ship to Nassau.¹⁰

For the second time within a week, Maffitt was guilty of violating regulations by entering port without permission. This was also a new regulation, and Governor Bayley readily accepted his apology and granted the *Florida* permission to remain there for twenty-four hours to take aboard the needed coal.¹¹ The ship was well received in Nassau, and according to Maffitt, a large majority of the population was openly pro-Confederate. The officials were very friendly and were most interested in the ship, which was visited by many officers from the British navy and the West Indies regiment.[12] While at Nassau, twenty-six men deserted from the *Florida*, but Maffitt was not greatly concerned about the loss.[13] This depletion was somewhat offset by six new recruits, whom he believed were first rate and perhaps worth more than those he had lost all put together. The *Florida* completed her coaling at 6:00 a.m. on January 27, and left port at 11:00 a.m. Maffitt took his ship outside the harbor and came to anchor where he waited until dark to get underway again, thus foiling any attempt by the United States authorities at Nassau to guess his course.[14]

On February 1, the *Florida* sighted an American sidewheel war steamer which was believed to be the *Santiago de Cuba*, a ship of ten guns. Since the *Florida's* mission was raiding commerce, Maffitt did not feel justified in risking her in combat, and thus he decided to run. The Federal warship gave chase and gained ground; however, each time the enemy came into range, she seemed to have engine trouble and fall back. When Maffitt learned later that his pursuer was not the *Santiago de Cuba* but the *Sonoma*, of only four guns, he was very sorry indeed that he had not engaged her.[15] According to Commander T. H. Stevens of the *Sonoma*, the Confederate ship was a much better sailer. Time and again, he would nearly catch the *Florida* only to have the wind increase, and Maffitt would regain the lead. There was no defect in the *Sonoma's* engines, as it had appeared to Maffitt, and Stevens was positive he could have outsteamed the Confederate ship had the wind not aided her.[16] It is likely neither Maffitt nor Stevens wished an engagement, Maffitt because any damage done to his ship would be difficult to repair, and Stevens because his vessel was outclassed by the

Florida. The chase lasted two days and was followed by five days of heavy seas, during which time the *Florida* was forced to keep up steam. This resulted in a frightful drain on her coal supply, and it was necessary once more to search for a port where fuel could be obtained. Maffitt was greatly disappointed that the coal shortage forced him to change his plan to make a raid on the coast of New England. In order to do that he needed a full supply.

On February 5, the *Florida* again missed destruction by only the greatest of luck. About 8:00 p.m. on this misty night, a very large steamer was sighted off the starboard beam of the cruiser. Apparently, the stranger sighted Maffitt's ship about the same time for she changed her course and steamed toward the Confederate at great speed. The *Florida* cut her steam and lowered her funnels, which were hinged and could be laid flat on the deck, disguising the fact that she was a steamer. The strange vessel, which Maffitt believed to be the *Vanderbilt,* one of the largest and fastest ships in the Federal Navy, circled the *Florida,* and after apparently classifying her as a West India trader, she steamed away.[17] This was the height of irony since the *Vanderbilt,* which was at that time searching for the *Florida,* lost the opportunity to destroy her enemy by failing to recognize her. Once the bad weather ended, Maffitt was again able to operate his ship under sail and save the remaining coal for emergency use. He was fortunate that only one ship was sighted during the next several days, and she proved to be British.[18]

Late in the afternoon of February 12, the *Florida* captured the clipper ship *Jacob Bell* of New York. This vessel was the most valuable prize the Confederate cruiser captured during her entire career, with a cargo reputedly worth one and one-half million dollars.[19] The *Jacob Bell* was bound from Foochow, China, to New York with a cargo of 1380 tons of choice tea and 10,000 boxes of fire crackers.³⁰ She carried forty-three persons, including two women, all of whom were brought on board the *Florida*. The women were placed in the captain's cabin, and every effort was made to make them comfortable. Nevertheless, one of the women, a Mrs. Williams, who later wrote a book about her experiences, claimed she had not been well treated, and Maffitt and his men had plundered her personal baggage. Maffitt refuted Mrs. Williams' claim in his journal and referred to her as "something of a Tartar." Many years later, after reading her book, he wrote of the incident as follows: "Mistaking Mrs. Williams for a lady, I gave her the entire possession of my stateroom and slept on the qr. [quarter] deck between the guns." Captain Frisbie of the *Jacob Bell* must have shared Maffitt's estimation of the woman because in his report Frisbie wrote, "She is an awful woman—a perfect she devil!" Captain Frisbie's wife was the other woman who was aboard the *Jacob Bell*.³¹ A prize crew under Lieutenant Hoole was sent aboard the vessel and the two ships kept company over night. The following morning was spent in removing baggage and stores from the captured ship, and at two in the afternoon she was burned.

After this latest capture, the *Florida* cruised for several days without any significant incident. One sail was sighted and chased on February 15, but she escaped after dark. On the 17th, Maffitt was able to relieve the terribly crowded condition of his ship by persuading the captain of the Danish ship *Morning Star* to transport his prisoners to St. Thomas. The next few days were uneventful, and on February 24, the Confederate ship arrived at the harbor of Bridgetown, Barbados. Remembering the twenty-six men who deserted at Nassau. Maffitt held all his officers on duty and his men on board the ship.[22] He was impressed by the interest which the people of Barbados showed in the *Florida*. Apparently, she was the first Confederate warship to visit the port and, as a result, aroused much curiosity. Maffitt also believed that most of the people were pro-Confederate. He considered them much more friendly to the *Florida* than they had been when he visited there on the U.S. Frigate *Macedonian* many years before the war.[23]

Maffitt visited Barbados Governor James Walker and requested permission to obtain coal for his ship. Walker was not sure what action he should take since the *Florida* had obtained fuel in a British port less than ninety days before. To give Maffitt this privilege would violate the ninety day rule, but since it contained a provision excepting ships in dire need, Walker permitted Maffitt to convince him that because of the inclement weather, the ship was indeed in dire need of coal. This matter settled, Walker entertained Maffitt at an official dinner, where he was extremely well received by the guests who composed most of the important military and governmental officials on the island. Maffitt noted that after this, the *Florida* was visited by nearly all the army officers stationed in Bridgetown, the most of whom displayed pro-Southern sentiments.[24] During the evening, a number of merchants, supposedly friendly to the Confederacy, came on board and were entertained. He later admitted in his journal that not all these merchants were as benevolent as they had appeared, and three of them were caught trying to steal one of the *Florida's* small boats. This party was apparently well supplied with alcoholic beverages, since Maffitt spent many lines in his journal apologizing for drinking too much and promising himself not to drink any more while in command of the *Florida*.[25]

As was the usual practice, the United States Consul at

Bridgetown, Edward Throwbridge, made a protest to the governor for allowing the *Florida* to take on coal. Apparently, Throwbridge was not aware that the Confederate ship had violated the three months rule or doubtless his protest would have been stronger. He, nevertheless, questioned the British position of permitting the *Florida* to obtain one hundred tons of coal which was far more than she needed to reach her stated destination of Charleston. Throwbridge also requested that the *Florida* be detained in port so that two United States mechant ships there could escape. His request was granted, and the cruiser's departure was delayed for twenty-four hours. This turn of events delighted Maffitt, who needed the additional time to complete the supplying of his ship.[26] Doubtless Throwbridge had no idea he was doing Maffitt a favor by this action.[27] As was the case with all United States consuls, Throwbridge alerted the others in the area that the *Florida* was at Bridgetown and requested that all available warships be notified.[28]

Throwbridge's protest concerning the *Florida* was continued at the highest levels. William H. Seward, who was aware of the ninety day violation, protested the incident, saying that as far as he and President Lincoln were concerned, the action of the British government was not in any way justified, especially the waiving of the three months rule. Seward said the *Florida* was a pirate and was not due to receive any consideration at all.[29] This definition of the character of the *Florida,* while not acceptable to the British, was typical of Seward's communications. Had he been successful in persuading the world to accept the cruisers as pirates, they would have been denied the use of foreign ports and would no longer have been a menace to Federal shipping.

The *Florida,* having completed the coaling operation, left Barbados on February 25, 1863. In addition to coal and supplies, ten men came aboard the ship there and were signed on the crew as soon as the ship was at sea.[30] While in port, Maffitt had discharged Third Assistant Engineer W. H. Jackson, who was considered totally incompetent for this duty. Charles W. Quinn, Second Assistant Engineer, had previously reported that Jackson knew nothing about the *Florida's* engines and, furthermore, did not appear interested in learning his job. Quinn not only considered Jackson incompetent, but he also believed the man was a menace to the safety of the ship because he had been responsible for damage done to the machinery on several occasions.[31]

The *Florida* continued to cruise, and on March 6, captured the clipper ship *Star of Peace* of Boston.[32] This ship of about 1,000 tons carried saltpeter for the Federal army and some other valuable cargo. The *Star of Peace,* stripped of provisions and valuables, was set on fire and used for gunnery practice. When the Confederate ship was about twenty miles from the burning prize, the saltpeter ignited. Maffitt described this as a magnificent sight, the sky being as bright as day even twenty miles away.[33] He reported that the morale of his crew had been greatly improved by this last prize because he had been careful to distribute the small stores captured to all the men.[34]

On March 12, 1863, the schooner *Aldabaran* from New York was captured. She was loaded with flour, provisions, and assorted merchandise bound for Marapanim, Brazil. Maffitt removed the captain and crew and some stores from the schooner before burning her. He stated that Captain Hand claimed to be pro-Southern and could not understand why his ship had to be destroyed, but he blamed the United States for fighting an unnecessary war for the Negro rather than the Union.[35] While the prize crew was stripping the *Aldabaran,* the *Florida* overhauled the British schooner

Laura Ann. Maffitt tried to persuade the *Laura Ann's* captain to take some of his forty prisoners, but he refused.[36] Later in the day he was able to prevail on another British ship to take ten of the prisoners, including the captains of the *Star of Peace* and the *Aldabaran*.[37]

As might have been expected, the captures made by the *Florida* and the *Alabama* were having a tremendous impact on the shipping interests of the United States, and had led to loud protests from American shippers and merchants, especially after the fate of the *Jacob Bell* became known. According to William H. Seward, most American merchants regarded the continued loss of such valuable ships "as indicating nothing less than the destruction of our national navigating interest."[38] A *New York Times* editorial accused the Navy of a lack of diligence in its efforts to catch the raiders. The editorial pointed out that while George Preble had been dismissed from the Navy because the *Florida* got into Mobile, no one had been disciplined for allowing her to escape. This article demanded action, and without calling his name, attacked United States Secretary of the Navy Gideon Welles as incompetent. The *Times* asked why the *Vanderbilt* had not been dispatched to search for the raiders, since she was one of the fastest ships in the Navy.[39]

From this statement, it is evident that the *Times* was not aware that the *Vanderbilt* was already in the area. Actually, the United States was trying desperately to eliminate the menace of the Confederate cruisers. Diplomatic pressure was constantly being applied through the consuls and ministers to foreign governments, especially the British. In addition to the diplomatic efforts of the Union, the Navy was doing what it could to capture or destroy the raiders. Welles, who was often blamed by the press for the failure to stop the cruisers, had many problems to consider. He had to maintain the blockade on the one hand and furnish ships for pursuit of the raiders on the other, and no matter what course he followed, he could not avoid criticism. The number of ships available was not adequate to accomplish all the tasks he was called upon to perform. Admiral Charles Wilkes, commander of the West Indian squadron, which was one of the main forces chasing the raiders as well as backing up the blockade, complained bitterly when Welles took the *Vanderbilt* and the *Dakota* away from him and assigned them to other duties. He protested that the only ships he had left were some small gunboats which were largely suited for river operations, and he doubted if they could defeat a raider even if they happened to apprehend one.[40] Public pressure supported Wilkes' demand for ships, and Welles was ultimately forced to countermand his order and allow the *Vanderbilt* to continue searching for the raiders. He also sent additional ships.[41] Welles, supported by Admiral J. F. DuPont and many of his officers, considered the Navy's main function was the maintenance of a strong blockade. These men believed, and rightly so, that the South could not continue to fight if the blockade were made tight enough to halt supplies. The raiders could damage the United States' cause, to be sure, but this would not result in the loss of the war. Therefore, it was more important to maintain the blockade than to search for the raiders.[42] Welles was forced ultimately to assign some ships for cruising duty, but his main objective was to keep the blockade at full strength at all times.[43] In retrospect, his decision seems to have been correct. The ships actually sent out to intercept the raiders realized little success considering the numbers engaged in this service, while the blockading ships were far more effective.

Maffitt continued his cruise after the capture of the *Aldabaran*, but he sighted few ships. On March 18, the

Florida stopped the British ship *Runnymead* and was able to persuade her captain to take eleven of the prisoners. Later, three more were placed on board an Austrian ship bound for New York. However, there was still another way of disposing of prisoners, and on March 21, two men taken from the *Star of Peace* were signed on the crew of the *Florida*. This was the first time Maffitt had allowed former prisoners to join his crew, but apparently the plan was successful because this practice continued for the remainder of the ship's career. Captured seamen enlisted on the *Florida* for a number of reasons. In the first place, the pay was better than could be expected in the merchant service, and considerable amounts of prize money were expected at the end of the war; secondly, when there were a large number of prisoners aboard, they had to be kept in irons and after a few days of such confinement, many were doubtless ready to sign on just to get the freedom of the ship; and finally, many of the crewmen were not Americans and had no loyalties as far as the war was concerned."

The United States bark *Lapwing,* carrying a cargo of good coal, was captured on March 28. Because of the coal, Maffitt resolved to use her for a tender, and since the sea was calm at the time of the capture, the Confederate ship was able to take ten tons of the fuel on board immediately. As an outfit for the prize, he sent three officers, including Lieutenant Averett, and fifteen men on board the *Lapwing*. A twelve pound howitzer was added for armament, and the ship was to be used as both a tender and a cruiser. Maffitt instructed Averett to cruise along the same course as the *Florida,* keeping from six to eight miles away. The Confederates hoped this extended view of the ocean would enable them to capture more prizes. Averett was furnished with a signal book and flags, and he was given two rendezvous points at which he could meet the *Florida* in the event the two ships became separated.[45] It was soon discovered that the *Lapwing* was not a good sailer and could not keep pace with the *Florida,* and as a result the two ships lost sight of each other after one day.[46]

On March 30, the *Florida* captured the bark *M. J. Colcord* of New York, a ship bound for Capetown with an assorted cargo. Maffitt spent most of the next day transferring provisions from the exceptionally well supplied prize. While the crew was still removing these provisions, the Danish ship *Christian* was stopped, and her master agreed to take all prisoners to Santa Cruz. Continuing her cruise, the *Florida* met the *Lapwing* on April 15, and two days were spent coaling the ship. Maffitt resumed his course after this interval and on April 17, captured the clipper ship *Commonwealth* of New York. This vessel was bound for San Francisco with an assorted cargo including about $60,000 worth of provisions owned by the United States government. The ship and cargo together were valued at $370,000, and its capture greatly pleased Maffitt.[47] The *Florida* took aboard what provisions she could and burned the *Commonwealth.* The bark *Henrietta* of Baltimore was captured and burned on April 23. She was bound for Rio de Janeiro with a cargo of 3250 barrels of flour and 600 kegs of lard.[48] The next seizure, made on April 25, was the clipper ship *Oneida* of New Bedford, a vessel from Shanghai, China, bound for New York with a large cargo of tea. Maffitt estimated that the *Oneida* and her cargo were worth around $1,000,000.[49] Captain James T. Potter was extremely bitter with Maffitt for destroying his ship before Potter could remove his clothing, and because he had to pay 400 francs to the captain of the French ship which took him and two of his officers as passengers.[50]

The *Florida* reached the Brazilian island of Fernando de Noronha about April 27, where she again met the *Lapwing*. Upon his arrival, Maffitt discovered he had missed the *Alabama* by one day; the sister ship had left the previous day. On May 1st, a Brazilian mail steamer brought in a new governor for the island. Maffitt reported that the old governor had been deposed because he had been too friendly to Captain Semmes of the *Alabama*.[51] The new governor, Colonel Antonio Gomez Leal, wasted no time in communicating with Maffitt and protesting the burning of ships carried out there by the *Alabama*. Since Maffitt had landed thirty-two prisoners on the island, Gomez believed he was planning to do the same thing, and so he ordered the *Florida* to take what supplies she needed but to be out of the port within twenty-four hours.[52] Not wishing to offend the Brazilians any further, Maffitt withdrew from Fernando de Noronha, towing the *Lapwing* to a quiet, uninhabited area near the island where he could take coal from her.[53] Some coal still remained aboard the tender, and she was sent to Rocas Island to wait for the *Florida*. Maffitt considered Rocas to be a safe place for the ships to rendezvous because it was uninhabited.

On May 6, the *Florida* captured the *Clarence* of Baltimore, a brig carrying a cargo of coffee. Lieutenant C. W. Read wished to take the ship, her cargo and papers and try to enter Hampton Roads, and if possible capture a gunboat or burn the shipping there. Maffitt agreed to Read's proposal, and thus the second "satellite" cruiser of the *Florida* was created.[54]

In a letter to J. D. Bulloch, Maffitt claimed his cruise so far, from January through April, 1863, had accounted for the loss of around six million dollars worth of American shipping and cargoes. Although this was a gross exaggeration of the damage, Maffitt was doubtless correct in saying that the Yankees were suffering in the pocketbook and "that touches them tenderly."[55] The cruise, especially that part conducted along the coast of Brazil, caused tremendous excitement in the United States. The *Florida* and the *Alabama* were both operating in Brazilian waters, and between them, they had destroyed a vast amount of American commerce, including at least twelve large ships of considerable value; among these were the *Commonwealth, Oneida,* and *Jacob Bell.*[56] This area between Rocas and Fernando de Noronha was the main track of American east coast-west coast shipping, far eastern shipping, Brazilian or South American shipping, and some African shipping. American merchants operating in these waters demanded that warships be dispatched at once and offered the Navy every facility at their disposal if it would break up these Confederate attacks. Passengers and crews of the captured ships were stranded in Brazilian ports, apparently because American merchant ships feared to leave.[57]

Actually, there was only one warship, the U.S.S. *Mohican,* commanded by O. S. Glisson, which had any chance of dealing with the raiders in the South Atlantic. This ship had followed the captures of the *Alabama* and *Florida,* and Captain Glisson believed he would eventually have an opportunity to engage at least one of the raiders and could sink her. He had been operating to the north but had come south to investigate the captures.[58]

It was difficult for the United States Navy to operate in the South Atlantic. In the first place, since their ships were far from any Federal naval bases, it was almost as hard for them to obtain coal and supplies and make repairs as it was for the Confederate raiders. The lack of communication was another hindrance. There was no direct mail service between the United States and Brazil. The mail came only once a month from Britain and France, and it was often a minimum of six weeks before any information of Confederate activities in that area could reach the Navy Department.[59]

There were other reasons for the lack of United States warships in the South Atlantic during the Spring of 1863. Federal Admiral Wilkes had kept his ships in the area of the British West Indian ports believing that the raiders would move into these ports in about May or June when their ninety-day limit on obtaining supplies had passed.[60] Wilkes' plan was agreeable to Welles since he had always wanted to keep the United States warships nearer the Southern coast in order to apprehend blockade runners. The reasoning was sound for the Confederates had in the past and would in the future do exactly as Wilkes predicted, namely, put into British ports for coal and repairs about every ninety days. However, this time he guessed wrong, at least in part. The Confederates did not come into these ports until later in the summer than Wilkes had supposed.

After outfitting the *Clarence,* the *Florida* continued her cruise toward Pernambuco, Brazil, arriving there on May 8, 1863. During the voyage, several ships were sighted but they were not American.[61] After extended negotiations with Joao Silverra de Sousa, Governor of Pernambuco, Maffitt obtained permission to remain in that port for four days, on the grounds that the *Florida's* machinery was in very poor condition and this length of time would be needed to repair it. The normal rule would have allowed the ship to remain there for only twenty-four hours. In his interview with the Governor, Maffitt observed that the man was very much afraid of the United States government. Silverra told Maffitt that he had received reports which indicated three Federal cruisers were supposed to arrive there in a few days; he doubted if Brazil could protect the *Florida*.⁶² Silverra's information was partially correct; one United States ship, rather than three, was on its way to Pernambuco and arrived there on May 20, several days after the *Florida* had put to sea. This ship, the *Mohican*, was, as has been noted, searching for the cruiser, but arrived too late to catch her.⁶³ During the four days the *Florida* was in this port, she was repaired and resupplied with coal and provisions, and the crew was given shore leave. On May 12, the *Florida*, having completed her repairs and supplying, left the port.⁶⁴

The United States Consul at Pernambuco, Thomas W. Adamson, protested the favors granted the *Florida*, especially that of allowing the Confederates to land their prisoners. Governor Silverra rejected this protest, insisting that the Confederate ship was being given exactly the same privileges which were extended to United States ships. With regard to the landing of the prisoners, Silverra said that this was done in the name of humanity and asked Adamson if he believed they should have been dumped into the sea.⁶⁵ In addition to his remonstrance, Consul Adamson also resorted to positive action to hamper the movements of Confederate raiders. He revoked the contract between the United States government and the British firm of Wilson and Company because this company had supplied coal to the *Florida*.⁶⁶ The practice of boycotting companies doing business with the Confederates seems to have been common during the Civil War, and there are several similar incidents in regard to the *Florida* on record.

J. Watson Webb, United States Minister to Brazil, also protested the favorable treatment given the *Florida* in Pernambuco, and in addition to repeating Adamson's charges, Webb complained that the officers and crew of the cruiser had been allowed to sell goods which had been captured from United States ships. Webb pointed out that this was a violation of international law, since these goods constituted part of a prize.[67]

The day after leaving Pernambuco, the *Florida* captured the *Crown Point,* a Boston ship bound to San Francisco from New York, with 1100 tons of assorted cargo of great value. According to the statement of John E. Norman, third officer of the *Crown Point,* the *Florida* was flying the British flag and appeared to be a British warship. Norman considered this action an offense against Britain since the Confederate flag was not raised until the prize crew was actually coming aboard. After the transfer of the passengers and crew, the *Crown Point* was stripped and burned.[68] The *Florida* then proceeded to Rocas Island to meet the *Lapwing.*[69]

After the *Lapwing* became separated from the *Florida,* she began a cruise of her own. Lieutenant Averett chased several ships, but he was unable to apprehend any that were American. On April 15, the *Florida* was sighted once more, a meeting which Maffitt described in his journal as a "godsend," because he was almost out of coal.[70] He was pleased to find all on board the prize were in good health and living like kings on "Yankee plunder." Averett was unhappy because the *Lapwing* had not been able to take any prizes as a result of her lack of speed. There was no absence of zeal on the part of the officers and men on board. Upon learning of the *Lapwing's* poor sailing qualities, Maffitt resolved to burn her as soon as all the coal was unloaded. In the meantime, he revoked all of Averett's orders and instructed him to meet the *Florida* at Fernando de Noronha on May 4; the two ships parted company again.[71]

On this voyage, the *Lapwing* had better luck and was able

to capture the *Kate Dyer,* an American ship carrying a neutral cargo from Antwerp. Midshipman Terry Sinclair, who served on the *Lapwing,* explained that this capture was made by a ruse. Most ships were not afraid of the *Lapwing's* twelve pound gun and often took to flight when a warning shot was fired. Since the prize was so slow, most of the enemy vessels simply sailed off and left her. This time, however, the men took a spar, painted it black, and mounted it on the wheels of a carriage which had been found aboard. They then partly covered the "quaker" gun with canvas, leaving just enough visible to give the enemy an idea of what it was. When the *Lapwing* fired a shot across the stern of the *Kate Dyer,* her captain observed the large, partly covered gun and halted his ship. This captain was most provoked with himself when he discovered the truth, but by this time he was a prisoner.[72] Because of her neutral cargo, Averett bonded the ship for $40,000.[73]

The practice of bonding ships was used by all Confederate cruisers when for one reason or another, they did not wish to destroy their prizes. Prizes were normally bonded for one or more of the following reasons: first, if the ship carried neutral cargo and could prove it; second, if the prize had too many passengers on board and the raider was unable to accommodate them all; or, third, the raider might find she was carrying too many prisoners and, therefore, bond a small prize to load with prisoners. A bond was a signed statement by the captain of the prize stating that the ship had been captured, and that the owners would pay the Confederate government a certain sum for the release of the ship. This sum was based on the value of the ship and was to be paid at the end of the war. Although these bonds were never paid because of the Confederate defeat, most ship owners believed they would have to be paid and considered that they represented a great loss of property.[74]

After bonding the *Kate Dyer,* the *Lapwing* continued to cruise but caught no more American ships. The *Florida* was sighted off Fernando de Noronha on April 27. At this meeting Maffitt removed the howitzer and most of the personnel from the ship.[75] He ordered acting master R. S. Floyd to take her to Rocas Island eighty miles west of Fernando de Noronha and wait for the *Florida* so that the transfer of the remaining coal could be completed and the *Lapwing* burned.[76] Floyd sailed to what he believed was the rendezvous point where he waited for thirty days, eventually running short of supplies. When he could wait no longer, he sailed the ship to Barbados where he burned her just off shore on June 20, bringing his crew ashore in a small boat.[77] The officers and men of the *Lapwing* received an enthusiastic welcome and were entertained like royalty while at Barbados. They later took passage on a British ship, landing at Queenstown, Ireland, in July. The group then rejoined the *Florida* at Brest, France.[78]

In the meanwhile, the *Florida* was waiting at Rocas Island. During her stay, she sighted only one ship, which proved to be Danish, but at least Maffitt was able to persuade the captain to take ten of the *Florida's* prisoners.[79] The stay at the island was used in repainting the cruiser and making small repairs. Unfortunately, three men were lost during this time, one because of illness and two by drowning. The most serious loss was the drowning of Assistant Surgeon J. D. Grafton when a boat containing several officers was overturned.[80] After waiting for fifteen days, Maffitt decided the *Lapwing* had either been lost or captured. He left orders for her in case she appeared, and put to sea.[81] These orders were left in a bottle and a marker was placed to attract attention to them. It seems likely that the *Lapwing* was waiting near the wrong island. Otherwise, the two ships should have met. Maffitt then proceeded to Ceara, Brazil, where he was able to refill his coal bunkers, obtain provisions, and dispose of his remaining prisoners.

Thus relieved, the *Florida* put to sea and cruised on an eastward course, capturing the 900 ton clipper ship *Southern Cross* of Boston on June 6, 1863. The prize, bound to New York from the Pacific side of Mexico with a load of dyewood, was burned.[82] Six days later, Maffitt was able to send the captain, his wife, and the officers of the *Southern Cross* aboard the *Fleur de Para,* a French ship bound for Ceara.[83] On June 14, the *Florida* captured the clipper ship *Red Gauntlet* of Boston, bound to Hong Kong with a cargo of ice, coal, and musical instruments.[84] Maffitt removed the officers and crew of the ship and put aboard a prize crew which kept the two ships in company for several days in order that the *Florida* could receive the coal which was aboard the prize. Once the coaling operation was completed, the *Red Gauntlet* was burned.[85] The capture of this ship incited considerable protest on the part of her owners. The captain, A. H. Lucas, stated that the *Florida* flew the British flag and did not lower it until the prize crew was already on board his ship. Lucas also said most of his cargo belonged to British firms, and he had expected Maffitt to bond the ship, especially since he had British consular certificates proving his claim. According to Lucas, Maffitt said President Lincoln would not honor bonds, and he, Maffitt, planned to bond no more ships.[86] While Maffitt may have made this statement, he did, in fact, bond several more ships.

Secretary of State Seward made no immediate protest on the use of the British flag, but he stated in a dispatch to Charles Francis Adams that he was keeping a file on all these incidents for future action, indicating that he believed the British were to some degree responsible.[87] Considering the constant reports and the protests regarding the use of the British flag by the *Florida,* it seems evident that the claim was true.

The *Florida* continued her course eastward and on June 16 captured the *Benjamin F. Hoxie* of Mystic, Connecticut. This clipper ship bound from the west coast of Mexico to Falmouth, England, carried a cargo consisting of logwood and silver bars valued at $105,000.[88] Captain Carey claimed the cargo belonged to neutrals and, as a result, should not be destroyed.[89] Maffitt examined the ship's papers, but he believed them false, especially since the crew insisted that the cargo was American. He, therefore, removed the silver and burned the ship.[90] Upon reaching Bermuda, Maffitt delivered the silver bars to the firm of John T. Bourne, the Confederate agent there.[91] Later information proved that the silver did belong to an English firm, and in order to avoid trouble with the British government, the silver was shipped back to England and returned to its owners.[92] Secretary Mallory praised Maffitt for his action in capturing the *Hoxie* and the other ships but told him that in the future he should deposit all funds captured with the firm of Fraser, Trenholm and Company of Liverpool. Apparently, Mallory did not wish to have Bourne and Company involved in financial transactions of this nature.[93]

While the *Hoxie* was a valuable prize, she was certainly not as valuable as her captain claimed her to be. According to a report by Carey published in the *Royal Gazette* of Hamilton, Bermuda, his ship carried $400,000 worth of silver bars, thirty tons of silver ore, valued at $500,000, and $7,000 or $8,000 worth of gold.[94] This exaggeration of the value was probably an attempt by the irate Carey to stir British opinion against the *Florida*.

No American ships were sighted after the *Hoxie* for several days. On June 18, the Confederate cruiser overhauled the Italian ship *Due Fratelli*, bound from Montevideo to Falmouth, England, and Maffitt was able to persuade her captain to take some of his prisoners.[95] The next capture was the whaling schooner *V. H. Hill* of Providence, Rhode Island, on June 27.[96] Since this was not such a valuable ship and the *Florida* already had fifty-four prisoners, Maffitt bonded the *Hill* for $10,000 and placed all his prisoners on board.[97]

The course of the *Florida* at this time was toward the coast of the United States. On July 7, she captured the packet ship *Sunrise* from New York to Liverpool. Because this ship had a great number of passengers and a neutral cargo on board, Maffitt bonded her for $60,000. He learned from New York newspapers captured on the *Sunrise* that C. W. Read, who had been outfitted by the *Florida*, had already been raiding the coast of New England. As a result of this raid, a large number of United States cruisers had been dispatched to search the coast for Confederate ships. This information, plus the fact that his ship could not make full speed on the poor grade of coal taken from the *Red Gauntlet*, caused Maffitt to decide that it would not be safe to operate the *Florida* in the coastal waters of the United States for very long.

As if to confirm the fact that these waters were infested with Federal cruisers, the *Florida* sighted the U.S.S. *Ericsson* on July 8. This ship, which had been chartered and armed by the Navy, was out searching for Confederate raiders. Maffitt considered that the *Ericsson* could easily be captured by the *Florida*, so he ordered his ship cleared for action.[98] At the time he sighted the enemy, Maffitt was only about fifty or sixty miles from New York. The Confederate ship, in order to approach her adversary closely, showed British colors until she was well within range, at which time she ran up the Confederate flag and simultaneously gave the *Ericsson* a broadside. Apparently, the broadside panicked the green crew of the United States ship, and they ran from the after pivot gun seeking protection behind her bulwarks. The *Florida* could doubtless have finished her enemy or at least forced her to surrender with a few more broadsides. However, there arose a patch of fog, and before the Confederate raider could fire another broadside, the enemy had disappeared into it. When the *Ericsson* was seen again, she was five or six miles away, steaming at full speed toward Sandy Hook. The *Florida* tried to catch the Federal ship but poor coal and great distance doomed the chase to failure.[99]

The *Ericsson* had been sent out in search of the *Tacony* and was no match for the *Florida*. She carried a twenty-pound Parrott gun on pivot and two twelve-pound rifled howitzers on field carriages. The ship's commander, J. N. Miller, stated that he believed the *Florida* would have captured him if he had tried to engage her.[100] In a second report, Miller stated that he had originally thought the Confederate ship was the *Alabama* and only upon seeing her two smoke stacks did he realize she was the *Florida*.[101]

Maffitt, unable to apprehend the *Ericsson*, was forced to give up the chase because he was very near New York, and thus ended the *Florida's* only offensive action. However, the pursuit was not altogether fruitless. The Confederate ship captured the brig *W. B. Nash* bound from New York and the whaling schooner *Rienzi* from Provincetown with a cargo of oil. The *Nash* was captured first and burned. The crew of the *Rienzi*, seeing the burning *Nash*, abandoned their ship and took to the small boats. The *Florida* burned the

Rienzi also and headed for the open sea on a course which would eventually take her to Bermuda.[102]

It was fortunate for Maffitt and the *Florida* that he did not continue his course up the coast of New England. Gideon Welles had dispatched the *Tuscarora,* the *Shenandoah,* and four other steamers to cruise in the area of Nantucket in the hope of intercepting the *Florida.* Welles believed the cruiser was planning to meet the *Tacony* at that place.[103] While the *Florida* was not actually trying to meet the *Tacony,* she would have passed near Nantucket if she had continued northward. There is also the possibility that had she maintained that course, she might have fallen in with another of the lightly armed chartered vessels on the order of the *Ericsson* which she might have been able to capture and outfit as a cruiser.[104]

The *Florida* reached Bermuda on July 17, 1863, and the first duty was to bury J. L. Lynch, Assistant Paymaster, who had died of consumption. Maffitt had gone to Bermuda to obtain coal and make repairs, but he soon discovered there was no privately owned coal on hand.[105] He appealed to Governor George Ord to allow the ship to obtain a supply from the government stocks and also requested permission to use the government dockyard to repair his ship, since those facilities were believed to be the best on the island. Governor Ord refused both requests, but he did agree that Maffitt could obtain privately owned fuel and use any available commercial facilities to repair his ship. A coal ship was expected at any time, and Ord allowed the *Florida* to remain in port until a shipment arrived.[106]

On arrival at Bermuda, Maffitt had sent a message to the fort stating that he planned to salute the British flag and asked whether or not the salute would be returned. Colonel William Munro, the commander of the fort, after consulting the Governor, agreed that if Maffitt offered a salute, it would be returned gun for gun.[107] This incident is significant in that it was perhaps the only time the Confederate flag was thus saluted. In commenting on the incident and his general treatment, Maffitt considered the people and officials of Bermuda to be very friendly.[108]

Despite his delay, Maffitt obtained the necessary supplies and made emergency repairs on his ship, leaving Bermuda on July 25.[109] On August 6 the *Florida* captured the *Francis B. Cutting* bound for New York. This clipper ship, commanded by Captain James T. Maloney, carried 230 passengers, far too many for the Confederates to accommodate. Therefore, he bonded the *Cutting* for $40,000 and allowed her to proceed on her way.[110] Continuing the voyage, the *Florida* captured the clipper ship *Southern Rights* bound for New York with 400 passengers, and he also bonded this ship for $40,000.[111]

Because of her long cruise, the *Florida* was by this time in a bad state of repair. Maffitt had indicated at Bermuda that the ship needed to be put into drydock, but failing to obtain permission to use the government's docks there, he had made only temporary repairs. Both the engines and hull needed major reconditioning, and Maffitt wanted to put into an English port, but because of the British neutrality proclamation, the *Florida* would not be allowed there until October 26, 1863, a lapse of ninety days. On the other hand, the serious nature of the repairs needed made it imperative to take her to a major port and preferably one close to Britain so the necessary spare parts could be obtained easily. France was friendly to the Confederacy, so Maffitt chose a French Channel port. He selected Brest because it would be most difficult to blockade.

In order to make these arrangements, Maffitt landed Lieutenant Averett at Cork, Ireland, with orders to proceed to France, where he was to try to obtain permission to make the repairs at Brest. In this mission, Averett expected to have the aid of John Slidell, Confederate agent in France.¹¹² Reports that the *Florida* was in the channel and the landing of Averett and two other officers at Cork created a great deal of interest in England, and no doubt considerable anticipation among the American ships in English ports.¹¹³

On August 21, while cruising toward Brest, the *Florida* captured the ship *Anglo Saxon* of New York. The ship, carrying coal from Liverpool to New York, was burned in the English Channel. Maffitt tried to place his prisoners on board one of the several ships which he sighted in the channel, but he was not successful. He was at length forced to carry them into the port of Brest. This action led to a protest from the captured English Channel pilot, Evan Evans. Evans did not protest the capture, but he thought the *Florida* had no right to take him out of piloting grounds. He stated that he had asked Maffitt to place him on board a homeward bound English ship and Maffitt had refused. Evans was especially bitter at being landed in a foreign port, and he immediately entered his protest with the British Consul at Brest.¹¹⁴ Apparently, he did not realize or refused to admit that Maffitt had tried to place all the prisoners on board a ship bound for England. This capture so near British coastal waters caused the British Navy to dispatch warships into the channel to make certain British rights were not being violated.¹¹⁵

The *Florida* arrived at Brest on August 23, and was placed in quarantine until the next day. On August 24, Maffitt called on the admiral commanding the port where he was well received. The admiral informed him that although permission to put the *Florida* into drydock had not yet been received, he expected it to arrive at any time. Maffitt believed the over-hauling would require only about eighteen days, but this proved to be a great understatement.

The *Florida's* entry into the port at Brest ended the ship's first cruise, which had been most spectacular and certainly most profitable. The *Florida* had captured twenty-five prizes by her own action. Of these, nineteen were destroyed and six bonded. In addition to these prizes of the *Florida* herself, twenty-two ships were captured by the *Tacony, Clarence,* and *Lapwing,* "outfits" of the *Florida.* Of this group, fifteen were destroyed, six were bonded, and one, the *Archer,* was recaptured. A more detailed account of the *Clarence* and *Tacony* will be related subsequently. It can be said that the *Florida* directly or indirectly took forty-seven prizes during her first cruise.

Chapter Four

The Cruise of the *Clarence* and *Tacony*

No narration of the activities of the *Florida* would be complete without an account of her children. The *Clarence* and *Tacony* were directly or indirectly "outfits" of the *Florida,* and it, therefore, seems proper that their activities should be included in any chronicle of the ship. Their captures should be credited to her since she was responsible for their existence. The decision to outfit the *Clarence* as a cruiser rather than burn her outright proved to be one of the most fortunate moves made by the Confederacy. The great triumphs of the *Clarence* and her successor were the result of the imagination and audacity of her young commander, Lieutenant C. W. Read.

At the time the *Clarence* was captured, Read knew that Maffitt had under consideration the outfitting of another prize such as the *Lapwing.* Consequently, Read proposed taking the *Clarence* and proceeding to Hampton Roads where he hoped to be able to cut out a United States gunboat or steamer. While this would be a very dangerous plan, it was not believed impossible. The *Clarence* had proper papers showing her to be a regular United States merchant ship bound for Baltimore, up the Chesapeake Bay from Hampton Roads. The size of the crew which Read suggested placing aboard the prize was to be only twenty men, and this was not large enough to arouse suspicion. He believed the disguise would enable him to pass Fortress Monroe, and once past this barrier, he could either capture a warship or burn the shipping which would be anchored in Hampton Roads. He asked that he be allowed to take E. H. Brown, an engineer, and one of the firemen for the project. Maffitt would be able to replace Brown at Pernambuco, and Brown's health was such that he would soon have to be relieved from the *Florida* in any case.¹ After due consideration, Maffitt decided that Read's plan had some chance of success and he agreed to outfit the *Clarence*. He suggested that the young lieutenant might be able to cut out the *Sumpter,* a steamer which was anchored in an exposed position off Hampton Bay. Since the *Sumpter* was serving as a flagship, her capture would be greatly significant. Should this prove impossible, however, Read would at least be able to burn some of the shipping at Norfolk and make his way back to the Confederate lines through Burwell's Bay. Maffitt gave Read a howitzer and ammunition so that the *Clarence* could make captures on the way.²

The plan approved, Read took his twenty men on board the *Clarence* and set a course for the Capes of the Chesapeake Bay and Hampton Roads. He soon discovered that the *Clarence* was a slow ship, and although he sighted several ships near the Windward Islands, he was unable to apprehend any of them. In fact, because of the ship's lack of speed, he caught no prizes until June 6, when he overhauled the *Whistling Wind* of Philadelphia. This bark, bound for New Orleans with a load of coal for the Union Navy, was insured for $14,800 by the United States.³ Read burned the ship and expressed satisfaction that he was able to strike a blow to supplies bound for the forces of the United States.⁴ The day after his success with the *Whistling Wind,* Read took possession of the schooner *Alfred H. Partridge* of New York, one of the most unusual captures made by any of the Confederate raiders. This ship, bound for Matamoros, Mexico, was carrying a cargo of arms and clothing consigned to the Confederate forces in Texas. Read, apparently unaware of the existence of this kind of trade, was surprised at the nature of his prize and perhaps doubtful as to whether or not the cargo was actually bound for Texas. Thus, he made the captain sign a bond of $5,000 guaranteeing that he would deliver the cargo to the "loyal citizens of the Confederate States."⁵

On June 9, 1863, Read captured and burned the bark *Mary Alvina,* bound from Boston to New Orleans, carrying a cargo of commissary stores for the Union forces at New Orleans. Once again Read was able to strike directly at the United States government. He learned from newspapers aboard the *Mary Alvina* and from his prisoners that no vessels were allowed to enter Hampton Roads unless they carried government supplies. Even ships so engaged were boarded, carefully inspected, and placed under close guard while they were unloaded. He also learned, much to his disappointment, that the ships anchored near Fortress Monroe were guarded by one or more gunboats and there were numerous sentries on the wharf. From this information, he determined that it would be impossible to take his ship into Hampton Roads with any chance of completing his mission successfully.⁶

On the morning of June 12, Read captured the bark *Tacony* by using the subterfuge of flying the United States flag upside down, a distress signal. When Captain Munday of the *Tacony* brought his ship close to the *Clarence* to investigate, Read and his men lowered a boat and boarded the *Tacony*. Once on board, the Confederates drew revolvers and took charge of the vessel. While the prisoners were being removed from the prize, the schooner *M. A. Shindler,* bound for Philadelphia in ballast, drew alongside the *Clarence,* which was still flying the distress signal. Read's men boarded and captured the *Shindler* in exactly the same manner as the *Tacony.*[7]

An examination of the log of the *Tacony* revealed to Read that she was a faster ship than the *Clarence,* and so he resolved to burn the latter ship and use the new prize as a raider. While in the process of removing the howitzer from the *Clarence,* the Confederates sighted another ship passing close by. Since there were no guns on board the *Clarence,* the crew pointed one of their wooden dummy guns (quaker guns) at the newcomer and ordered her to heave to, which she did and was captured. This prize proved to be the schooner *Kate Stewart* sailing from Key West to Philadelphia in ballast. Since Read had over fifty prisoners, he decided to bond this latest prize and use her as a cartel, and after concluding the transfer, he bonded the ship for $7,000, about half her value.[8] Having rid himself of his prisoners, Read completed moving his men to the *Tacony* and burned the *Clarence* and *Shindler.*[9]

Within a short time, Read captured the *Arabella* of New York, a brig which was carrying a neutral cargo and could not be destroyed. He bonded her for $30,000, but no doubt regretted that he had not been able to transfer his prisoners to this ship so he could have destroyed the *Kate Stewart.*[10] With these releases, the presence of the raider off the coast of the United States was no longer a secret. This brought immediate pursuit, and Read had to be more cautious in his future operations.[11]

The *Tacony* captured the brig *Umpire* bound from Cardenas, Cuba, to Boston with a load of sugar and molasses. Read stripped and burned this ship and continued on his cruise. Five days later, on June 20, he captured the clipper ship *Isaac Webb* bound from Liverpool to New York with 750 passengers. Since he was unable to accommodate or make arrangements for the large number of passengers he was forced to bond the ship for $40,000.[12] He regretted that he could not burn her since she was a very valuable ship, and there is little doubt that her destruction would have caused serious repercussions for the United States Navy Department. The owners of the ship entered a violent protest over this capture even though the ship had not been destroyed. They felt that the Navy had been negligent in its duty.[13] On the same day of his encounter with the *Isaac Webb*, Read seized and burned the fishing schooner *Micawber*. The following day, he captured the clipper ship *Byzantium* bound from London to New York loaded with coal, and the bark *Goodspeed*, from Londonderry to New York in ballast. Both of these ships were stripped and destroyed.[14]

Read had decided by this time that the *Tacony* was becoming too well known, and perhaps he should look for another ship. He had examined the log of the *Goodspeed* to determine whether or not she had good sailing qualities, but apparently he was not satisfied. The owners of the *Goodspeed* and the *Byzantium* reported that their ships had both been passed by vessels of the United States Navy on the day of their capture, but neither merchant ship had been informed of the fact that there was a Confederate raider in the area. The owners were outraged by the failure of the

Navy to warn them of the danger of raiders. According to the protest, if the ships had been cautioned, they could easily have avoided capture. They also reported that Read boasted that he had burned two ships in sight of a United States gunboat. While this was not true, the ship owners accepted Read's statement as additional proof of the indifference of the United States Navy and demanded more protection.[15]

By June 22, the *Tacony* had reached the very heart of the fishing grounds. On that day, Read captured and burned the schooners *Marengo, Elizabeth Ann, Rufus Choate,* and *Ripple.* Since by this time he was carrying a number of prisoners, he bonded the old schooner *Florence,* the least valuable of his prizes, and placed seventy-five men on board. Once more Read cleared the *Tacony* of prisoners, but this was only temporary because the next day he destroyed two more fishing schooners, the *Ada* and the *Wanderer.*[16]

The following day Read captured the clipper ship *Shatemuc,* which was bound from Liverpool to Boston with 350 passengers. He was extremely anxious to burn this ship since she was loaded with iron plates and war supplies, and he spent most of the day vainly trying to catch fishing schooners so he could dispose of the passengers. Unfortunately for Read, this was an impossible task, and he was forced to allow the ship to proceed on her way after bonding her for $150,000.[17]

During the day, the *Tacony* had captured the fishing schooner *Archer.* This latter vessel was not large enough to accommodate the passengers and crew of the *Shatemuc,* but Read had another idea as to how to use his latest acquisition. He had expended all ammunition for his howitzer and, therefore, it would be impossible to make any more captures in the usual way.[18] He had also learned there were at least twenty gunboats searching for the *Tacony;* they were stopping every vessel that even remotely resembled her. Since he did not believe he could dodge his pursuers much longer, he resolved to transfer his crew to the *Archer*, which he described as a good sailing vessel of about ninety tons.[19] Perhaps no one would suspect that the *Archer* was a raider, and thus he could sail into some exposed harbor and either cut out a steamer, or burn shipping, or both.[20] To confuse the enemy even further on the location of the *Tacony*, he transferred to the *Archer* at night. The *Tacony* was then burned about 2:00 in the morning so that by daylight anything left of her had little resemblance to the elusive raider. Read hoped his pursuers would continue their search for the nonexistent ship.[21] He was correct in his assumption that there were a large number of Union ships looking for the *Tacony*. Welles reported that there were forty United States warships and chartered ships at sea in search of the raider.[22]

The consequence of Read's raids on the coastal commerce of the United States was to cause panic all along the Atlantic seaboard. Shippers demanded protection for their vessels as well as increased harbor defense. The sinking of the fishing boats probably provoked more concern than the other types of captures. Perhaps the dependence of such a large number of people along the coast of New England on the fishing industry gave these people more political power than the ordinary commercial shippers. In any case, their protests were stronger and more numerous than those of any other group, even though their vessels were less valuable. Actually, most of the fishing schooners were destroyed in a period of about four days, but this attack took place so quickly that no one was able to make a correct report. The press coverage of the raid on the fishing fleet was greatly exaggerated, and rumors added to the exaggeration. The *New York Times* reported that the *Tacony* had destroyed over forty fishing boats, when actually only seven were destroyed, one bonded, and the remaining one, the *Archer*, was recaptured at Portland, Maine.[22]

In spite of the gross exaggeration, the rumors were believed. Evidence of this can be found in the protests and demands for protection which came from all over New England. Several good examples will be cited here. Some thirty-two merchants of Boston sent a letter to Gideon Welles requesting protection for their fishing fleet. This request, while more reasonable than many, suggested that one or two armed sailing ships might be very well suited to protect the fishing fleet.[23] Another group suggested that regular warships should be stationed at the Grand Banks during the entire fishing season. This group pointed out that nothing prevented raiders from coming to the fishing banks at any time and with luck the raiders could destroy the entire fishing fleet in a few days if it were not guarded.[25] The most persistent request and certainly the most influential came from Massachusetts Governor John A. Andrew, who wanted some ships to guard the fishing fleet and commerce, and others to protect Boston harbor.[26] The Governor had, no doubt, been the recipient of much pressure because of the *Tacony's* raid. His protest stated that it had been reported to him that no warships were sent after the *Tacony* until she had spent four days making captures in the fishing grounds. Welles insisted that this was not true and said that the Navy was doing all it could. There is no doubt that the grievances against the Navy Department were great, in fact so great that Welles had no choice but to make some provisions for security of the harbors and coast of New England. Welles posted some ships and guns at Boston harbor and suggested that the Coast Guard might be able to supply defenses for some of the others.[27]

Not only was Welles faced with demands from New England but New York and other areas were also calling for security.[28] Perhaps one of the strangest requests for protection came from S. M. Felton asking that the Navy Department dispatch armed men and a gunboat to guard the ferry boat at Harve de Grace, Maryland.[29] Felton feared both a land and a sea raid on the ferry, which was of considerable importance since it was the railroad ferry and its destruction would have broken land communications on the East Coast. Welles apparently agreed that the ferry was important enough to be defended. He ordered a gunboat to be stationed there and two thirty-two pound guns to be installed on the ferry boat itself.[30]

It is clear that the Navy did not have enough ships to supply even a part of all that was requested, and it was still the department's basic policy that the first priority was a full-strength blockade. However, during Read's raid on the New England coast, the political pressure on Welles became so great that he was forced to compromise. He took some ships from blockade duty and also resorted to the expedient of chartering merchant vessels. These ships were armed, their officers given temporary naval commissions and sent out to search for the raiders or to protect special areas. This plan solved some of the problems faced by the Navy, but, at the same time, it drained off some of the trained manpower which was in such short supply. Also, it is doubtful if these ships would have accomplished much against a fully equipped raider such as the *Florida*. In spite of their short-comings, there were at least eight such vessels in use chasing the *Tacony*.[31] Welles apparently believed that the use of chartered ships would at least reduce some of the anxiety in the coastal area, even if the ships were not too effective against the raiders. He, therefore, offered to charter more vessels if they were available. What Welles really wanted was fast steam ships, since he considered they were the only class of vessels which could be of any real value against the raiders.[32]

Perhaps Read's high degree of success in his coastal raid can be attributed to three factors. First of all, the ships which were sent to search for him were one or two days behind, and instead of moving up the coast in an attempt to anticipate his movements, they would proceed into the area in which he had last been reported and begin their search there. This, of course, was useless since Read was far away by the time the search began.[33] Had he ever doubled back to any great extent and covered the same area twice, he would doubtless have been captured as there were great numbers of ships operating behind him.[34]

A second reason for the failure to capture Read was inaccurate reporting, as is true in most every period of public excitement. The *Tacony* was erronously said to have been sighted near Halifax, Nova Scotia, and that the ship was said to be a steamer.[35] On June 24 the master of the schooner *Le Roy* said that he had communicated with the *Kate Stewart* which reported that she had been boarded by the crew of the *Florida.* He went on to say that the *Kate Stewart* was carrying crews of prizes taken by the *Florida*. The captures were of course made by the *Tacony,* but here were the foundations for a good rumor. Fortunately, the Navy Department had been in direct communication with the *Kate Stewart* and realized the error, but similar reports were causing alarm and were responsible for sending warships in all directions.[36]

The third factor was that Read changed ships often; by the time he was reported to be in one type of vessel, he had changed to another. The *Clarence* was still being sought long after she had been exchanged for the *Tacony,* and the Navy was still looking for the *Tacony* when the *Archer* was finally captured.[37]

On the morning of June 26, Read sighted the Portland, Maine, lighthouse. He picked up two fishermen who, thinking that the group on board the *Archer* was a pleasure party, willingly piloted the vessel into Portland. Read, upon learning from the fishermen that both a passenger steamer to New York and the revenue cutter *Caleb Cushing* were in the harbor, decided immediately that the presence of these ships gave him exactly the opportunity he needed. He proposed to capture both the steamer and the cutter, but Brown, the only engineer, informed Read that he was not sure he alone would be able to start the engines of the steamer, and because of the short summer nights, the party might not have time to get away. Read, therefore, decided that since there was a good wind, it would be better to capture the *Caleb Cushing,* and after getting her out of the harbor to return with some of his men and set fire to the shipping. With this plan in mind, he and his men boarded the cutter at 1:30 a.m. and captured her with no noise or resistance.[38] To accomplish this plan, Read placed his men in boats with muffled oar locks and approached the cutter from both sides.

The deck watch of the *Cushing,* consisting of only two men, did not hear the boats until they were nearly alongside the cutter. They called out to Lieutenant Davenport, the officer in charge, but before he could reach the deck, the watch had been overpowered by men pouring over both sides of the vessel. The boarding party immediately went below and caught the remainder of the crew in their hammocks, and Lieutenant Davenport was captured as he came out of his cabin. The cutter's crew was then placed in double irons and held below deck.[39] Having secured the cutter, Read wasted no time in trying to get her underway. However, because of difficulty with the moorings, he was not able to do this until 2:00 a.m. In addition to this delay, Read discovered that the wind had died down and the tide was running against him.[40] In order to get the ship out of the harbor, he found it necessary to lower the boats and use them to tow the cutter.[41] This process was very slow, and the *Cushing* was not entirely clear of the harbor by daylight, but because Read had used an entrance which was unprotected, he was not fired upon.[42] Actually, the loss of the cutter was not discovered until 8:00 a.m. so there was little danger of her being fired upon in any case since no alarm had been given.

Upon hearing that the cutter was no longer at her anchorage, Jedediah Jewett, Collector of Customs at Portland, thought there was some kind of foul play. He believed that Lieutenant Davenport, of the *Cushing,* a Southerner who had remained in Federal service, might be responsible for it. The Customs Collector chartered the steamer *Forest City,* a 700 ton side wheeler, and sent to Fort Preble and Camp Lincoln for men and guns to put on board the steamer. The Mayor of Portland, also fearing foul play, had persuaded the captain of the steamer *Chesapeake* of New York to get up steam. Jewett placed two six-pound guns on board the *Chesapeake* and two twelve-pounders on the *Forest City,* manning these guns with troops from Fort Preble and Camp Lincoln. This armada, in the company of several tugs, left port in pursuit of the cutter.[43] When the cutter was some twenty miles out of Portland, Read observed two large steamers and three tugs coming out of Portland in pursuit. He immediately ordered the cutter cleared for action, and as soon as the leading steamer came into range, he opened fire with the cutter's thirty-two pounder.[44] After several near misses, the captain of the *Forest City* withdrew his ship and waited for the *Chesapeake* to catch up. It was then decided that the *Chesapeake,* since she was a propeller steamer and had fifty bales of cotton on board for barricades, should run the cutter down. The cutter then opened fire on the *Chesapeake* with three or four shots, the last of which was shrapnel.[45]

After the fighting began, Read made a very unfortunate discovery. He was able to locate only five projectiles for the pivot gun and believed these were all that were on board the cutter. His next move was to fire several rounds of shrapnel, which did not stop the steamers. He then ordered his men to abandon ship and set the cutter afire.[46] The prisoners were in one boat, and Read used two others for his own men. The Confederates were picked up by the *Forest City* and the prisoners by the *Chesapeake.* The cutter, which was by this time burning all over, had 500 pounds of powder on board and as a result was considered too dangerous to try to salvage.[47] After he learned from the Confederate prisoners that they had come to Portland in the *Archer,* the captain of the *Forest City* sailed eastward looking for that vessel which he captured at about 2:00 p.m.[48]

In later reporting on this action, Jewett stated that the cutter had a thirty-pound gun on pivot aft and a twelve-pound gun on pivot forward. He said that had Read found the cutter's shot locker, she would have been very dangerous, since there were, in fact, ninety rounds of shot on board the cutter. Jewett believed the *Chesapeake* would have tried to run down the cutter had she continued to fight, and this would have probably caused her to sink with considerable loss of life. Had Read been able to continue, the *Chesapeake* might have run down the cutter as Jewett suggested, but it is much more likely the cutter would have made good her escape. The civilian captains, as was the case of the captain of the *Forest City*, had no desire to get close to Read's thirty-two pounder, which with competent gunnery could have sunk both ships. Doubtless the real heroes of this fight were Davenport and his crew, who refused to reveal the location of the *Cushing's* shot locker.[49]

After having been sent as a prisoner to Fort Preble, Read had to request that money be sent him so he could buy his men a change of clothing. It seems all spare clothing had been distributed to the people of Portland as souvenirs.[50] Read was perhaps fortunate that he lost only his clothing, since there was for a time some question as to whether he and his men were prisoners of war or pirates.[51]

With this action, Read's raid was put to an end, but not before it had taken twenty-one prizes, burning fifteen, and caused panic along the entire coast of the United States north of Norfolk. All of this was done by twenty men and one young officer who was only twenty-three years old at the time. This remarkable man, who planned the entire operation, had the reputation of being slow witted and a bit of a dreamer. He had, in fact, been the "anchor man" of the Class of 1860 at the United States Naval Academy, graduating twenty-fifth in a class of twenty-five. While at the Naval Academy, he had been called "Savey" Read because of his low marks.[52] In any case, it is seldom in recorded history that so few men have been able to do so much damage to an enemy. Reed and his men were certainly the most profitable military investment ever made by the South, and his coastal raid against New England was not the end. Read was exchanged in 1864 and again distinguished himself in the Red River Campaign.

Chapter Five

The *Florida* at Brest

WHEN THE "FLORIDA" arrived in Brest Bay on August 23, 1863, Maffitt immediately sought permission to refit and resupply the ship. The vessel needed considerable work on her engines, copper sheathing and general overhauling. Vice Admiral Count de Gueyton, who was in charge of the port at Brest, informed Maffitt that the ship would be given the same rights and privileges as the merchant ships which came into the harbor. She could take on any or all supplies she wished and make use of any privately owned facilities needed in order to complete necessary repairs, but she would not be allowed to increase her armament.'

Within a few days after the ship's arrival, it was determined that the commercial resources of the port would not be sufficient to make the repairs. Maffitt, therefore, called on de Gueyton once more. This time he asked for permission to use the government dockyard since these were the only facilities available for properly repairing the vessel. The French agreed to this request provided the expense would be promptly paid. It was necessary also for all munitions to be removed from the ship before she would be allowed to enter the dock, a task accomplished by loading them on a barge anchored alongside the Confederate. After these details were settled, a M. Aumaitre, agent of the *Florida* at Brest, made the financial arrangements, and the ship was taken into the government dockyard.[2] The extent of the overhaul known to be needed at this point was such that Aumaitre required Maffitt to make a deposit of 40,000 francs in advance.[3] According to the British consular report, the work ultimately cost 135,000 francs and the cost of maintaining the ship, crew, etc., while in Brest was over 300,000 francs.[4]

United States Minister to France William L. Dayton was quick to protest this action by the French government, insisting that the *Florida* was, in truth, a piratical vessel. Dayton anticipated that the French government would consider the cruiser a ship of war belonging to a belligerent, but he thought they still ought not to allow her to make more than minor repairs and only those considered necessary to permit her to put to sea. Although Maffitt had wished to overhaul the machinery of the ship, Dayton thought it would be perfectly safe for the *Florida* to put to sea with her sail which was in good condition.[5]

When the French gave permission to the *Florida* to use the government dockyard, Dayton again protested and implied that this was anything but neutral conduct.[6] However, considering the usual vehemence of American protests concerning any aid to the cruiser, this one seemed relatively mild. An explanation can perhaps be found in a statement made by John Bigelow, United States Consul at Paris, in a letter to Henry S. Sanford, United States Minister to Belgium; Bigelow wrote,

"I hope they will let the *Florida* into the Government Docks. I will engage that she does not get out in four or five months. All her machinery will have to be taken out of her piece by piece and nothing is quite so slow as a French Government work shop of any kind."[7]

Considering the length of time taken to refit the *Florida*, Bigelow's idea appeared to be correct. Early in September, several French ship owners obtained an order from the Tribunal of Commerce at Marseille to seize the *Florida* for damages which these men claimed the Confederate ship had done to their property. One ship owner, M. Merrier, claimed damages of 100,000 francs for one of his ships seized by the *Florida* and forced off its course to carry prisoners to Acapulco, Mexico. Another owner claimed he had lost cargo on the *W. B. Nash*, which had been burned.[8] These claims were not made at the instigation of the United States government; in fact, Dayton reported to Seward that he thought it best for them to stay out of this affair since it would have a better chance without United States interference.[9] Bigelow considered that seizure of the ship would hurt the Confederacy, and the only legal way France could refuse to seize the ship was to recognize her as a regularly constituted warship. Such recognition of the *Florida* would prove to be a great source of embarrassment for the French government and would result in considerable agitation among the French citizenery.[10]

Despite the hopes and expectations of Dayton and Seward, the seizure of the *Florida* was disallowed. The French Minister of Marine refused to accept the claims, stating that they were made against a recognized belligerent, and since the *Florida* was a man of war, she could not be seized. He pointed out also that the United States had not agreed to the Declaration of Paris against privateering, and damages could not be obtained for neutral goods destroyed on United States ships.[11]

The effect of the seizure and release of the ship, except for raising the hopes of the Federals and perhaps angering some French merchants at their own government, was nil. Nor does it appear that the serious agitation predicted by Bigelow over recognition of the ship as a man of war materialized. Certainly, whatever agitation occurred did not seriously impair relations between France and the Confederacy. Apparently, the repairs on the ship were not even stopped when she was seized. In fact, it is not clear whether or not the seizure order was ever served on the *Florida*.[12]

In addition to the protest over permitting repairs for the *Florida*, the representatives of the government of the United States were using every pretext which they could muster to get the ship seized, delayed, or captured while she was at Brest or as soon as she left that port. Not satisfied with earlier rejections, Dayton made a second and much stronger protest with regard to the nature of the *Florida*, which he still insisted was a privateer. He censured the French for permitting the ship to refit at Brest, since they had agreed in the Declaration of Paris not to respect privateers.[13] He explained that it was the contention of the United States that a commerce raider was a privateer whether she carried a letter of marque or a commission.[14] The French rejected this claim and insisted that since the ship had a commission, she was a warship and was entitled to make any navigational repairs she wished so long as there was no increase in her armament. They further explained that even if the *Florida* had been a privateer, she could legally refit in a French port. They re-emphasized that while France had signed the Declaration of Paris, the United States had not and, therefore, was not entitled to any protection from it.[15] The French rejected both the United States' protest and their definition of privateers.

Along with these protests, the United States used some threats. Seward suggested that if France, a maritime nation, did not cease aiding the Confederate raiders, the United States would be justified in reciprocating in future wars. He reminded the French that America would make an excellent base for privateers operating against French commerce.[16] Another threat used on France to prevent continued aid to the South was the stoppage of the tobacco trade. The French had been allowed a special license to bring tobacco through the blockade, a practice which could easily have been eliminated.[17]

The repairs made on the *Florida* were extensive. She entered the government dockyard on the ninth of September, 1863, where she remained for about five weeks. After this, the ship was moved to the merchant harbor of Brest, where she was slowly refitted, not being moved into the roadstead until December 27, and even then not all the work had been completed.[18] One reason for the long delay and great cost involved in repairing the cruiser was that her engines were of British manufacture. The French mechanics were not familiar with these engines and it was necessary to bring mechanics and many spare parts from Britain, a turn of events which prolonged the task much more than anticipated. The French permitted the *Florida* to remain in port as long as was necessary and to bring from Britain whatever men and materials were needed, provided all tariffs were paid on the new equipment.[19] These repairs were doubly expensive to the Confederacy for not only was the cost of the work tremendous but there was also the additional expenditure of maintaining the ship and her crew in port. The *Florida* had yet another disappointment. After all these months of waiting, the ship was taken on trial runs through the harbor on January 25 and 27, 1864, only to discover that additional work was needed. This entailed another delay of about ten days.[20]

While at Brest, the *Florida* added a blower system to the boilers, for which all equipment had to be sent from Britain. This system was expected to give her greater speed and enable her to burn low grade coal. However, the trial trip proved that the blower did little to add to her speed, since the engines were not built to withstand the increased revolutions and the vibration would soon cause them to fail. The blower, no doubt, did enable the *Florida* to use low grade coal, but was effective in increasing her speed only in an emergency.[21] In spite of the work done at Brest, the ship was never again able to make more than eight knots under steam alone.[22] This was considerably less than she had made during her first cruise and would indicate that even though a great deal of time and money had been expended on her the tremendous repair and overhaul project was not entirely satisfactory.

Nothing was done to increase the number of the *Florida's* guns, but the Confederates requested that they be allowed to land the heavy guns of the ship for repairs on their machinery. The French did not accede to this, though they did allow mechanics to work on board[23] and permitted the small arms to be taken ashore to a gunsmith provided no ammunition or additional small arms were purchased.[24]

The *Florida* was able to obtain new gun tackle, about 500 fuses for her shells and a large quantity of other equipment for her ordnance, but her total battery was not increased. This material, although ordered while at Brest, was not actually loaded at that port.[25] It was delivered to the ship at sea near Belle Isle on February 19, as related later.[26] While the ship was in port, there were constant reports that she was receiving new guns on board. F. H. Morse, United

States Consul at London, said that two new Berkley rifles had been shipped from London for the cruiser.[27] His statement naturally led to a protest to the French government, but there was no truth in the rumor, since these guns were never placed on the *Florida*. It may have been that they were bound to the *Georgia* or the *Rappahannock,* both of which were also in French ports at that time making repairs and filling up their crews.[28]

Seizure and diplomatic protests were not the only problems faced by the *Florida* while stationed at Brest. Her able commander, Maffitt, asked to be relieved from duty because of ill health. Maffitt explained to his family that he had had a recurrence of his old heart ailment and had been ordered by the doctor to take at least three months rest. He seemed to believe his illness was the result of his bout with yellow fever during the previous year and exhaustion from the strenuous eight months of command.[29] Although the work on the ship may not have been retarded by this action as Maffitt was not relieved until September 17, after the *Florida* had been placed in the government docks, it is likely that the confusion caused by this change of command lead to some delays in later affairs of the ship.

Perhaps the most vexing situation for the *Florida* at Brest concerned her crew. Soon after putting into port, Maffitt discharged fifty-nine men.[30] The records are not entirely clear as to why this action was taken since part of the ship's log for this period has been lost. One reason may have been financial. The cost of maintaining so many men in idleness would have been enormous. According to the account of G. Terry Sinclair, a midshipman on the *Florida,* Maffitt allowed the officers shore leave to go to Paris soon after the ship reached Brest, and because of a rumor that the crew was to be kept on board ship, there was a mutiny. Sinclair reported that all the men involved in this fracas were discharged even though many were repentant upon learning the truth. This incident may very well have been the reason for discharging so many men, but it is doubtful if it was as serious as Sinclair described. No mention of this appeared in any dispatch of the American officials who were watching the *Florida,* and certainly they would have been quick to report such a happening. The credibility of Sinclair's account is also considerably weakened by the fact that it was not related until thirty-five years later.

An examination of the existing portions of the ship's log for the time she was at Brest seems to lend credence to the idea that discipline was a major problem. There were numerous notations of men being confined for every kind of offense from insolence and theft to leaving the ship without permission.[31] This type of conduct was very rare on the ship prior to her arrival at Brest and idleness must have been a major cause. Some of the crew doubtless would have remained under Maffitt if he had returned to that command. In fact, a petition was signed by fourteen crewmen requesting transfer to whatever ship he commanded.[32] In addition to this petition, there is evidence that the men disliked the junior officers, especially Lieutenant Averett, and that this was a major reason for wanting to leave the ship. This is clearly stated in several letters written to Maffitt by various members of the crew at a later date.[33]

Discharging a major portion of the crew proved to be unfortunate. These were experienced men, largely recruited at Mobile, and they had to be replaced by inexperienced seamen enlisted with great difficulty from all over Europe. The second crew did not attain the skill and efficiency of the first until near the end of the voyage, nor was their *esprit de corps* as high as that of the first crew.

When these men left the *Florida,* Maffitt gave each one twenty-five dollars on account and arranged for passage to Liverpool. Their remaining wages were to be paid by Fraser Trenholm and Company when the men reached England. Unfortunately, when they arrived there, they found that Fraser Trenholm and Company had not received any letter from Maffitt authorizing payment.[34] What had actually happened was that Maffitt had sent all accounts and records to Confederate agent James D. Bulloch, who was to make the arrangements with the company.[35] This letter and the records were to be delivered to Bulloch by one of the crew members, but when the men arrived in Liverpool, Bulloch was out of the city and could not be found. This situation caused serious repercussions. After about five days of waiting, some of the men, impatient and believing they had been cheated, went to the office of the American Consul at Liverpool. These men showed Thomas Dudley the letter from Maffitt as well as a list of the men who had been discharged. In fact, Dudley was allowed to make copies of these documents.[36] The men, doubtless at Dudley's suggestion, placed the following note in the Liverpool *Daily Post :*

"We the undersigned sailors and firemen of the steamer *Florida,* wish to know if Captain Bulloch, agent of the Confederate States of America, will pay our orders from Captain Maffitt, Commander of the Confederate States steamer *Florida,* as we have now been here five days, and have no means of subsistence. We trust that Captain Bulloch will send his address to 36, Sparling Street. We have all got orders for our wages from Captain Maffitt, amounting to from $60 to $260 each, and we trust that we shall have no further trouble getting our money."[37]

This notice was the last mention of pay in the public press, and, according to the statement of William Thompson, a coal heaver from the *Florida,* the wages were paid in full on September 29, 1863.[38]

The significance of this incident was that it undoubtedly added to the difficulty of recruiting a new crew, but even more important was the fact that the United States had gained possession of a list of former crew members of the *Florida.* This enabled Charles F. Adams to protest the recruiting of British subjects and present a list showing that many of these men were, in fact, citizens of Britain. Adams stated that as far as he was concerned this list proved without question that there had been a violation of that part of the Foreign Enlistment Act which prohibited the recruiting of British nationals. Adams also warned that a number of these men were believed to be bound for new Confederate ships which were being built in Britain.[39] Another roster which had come into Adams' possession was a select list of fifteen men from the *Florida* who had requested transfer to other Confederate ships.[40] From these lists, United States officials discovered four "ex-Floridians" had joined the crew of a British ship bound for New York, and plans were made to deal with the men when they reached that port.[41]

The *Florida's* lack of men for her crew delayed her departure from Brest, and although the French agreed that the discharged men could be replaced, they insisted that French nationals could not be enlisted and thus made recruiting extremely difficult.[42] This might not have been an insurmountable problem had the Confederate agents been able to operate freely in British ports, but agents of the United States, realizing that most men for the ship would come from Britain, did all in their power to prevent prospects from signing on the Confederate ship. One method used successfully by the Federal agents was to locate all men in Liverpool and other port cities of Britain who were believed to be interested in enlisting on the *Florida* and pay them full wages to remain at home. Wherever American agents were able to locate the men, this plan seemed to have worked very well, even though it cost considerable money.⁴³ Another means of discouraging the recruiting of crews in Britain was to prosecute under the Foreign Enlistment Act both the Confederate agents and the men whom they were enrolling. These prosecutions, successful or not, had a dissuading effect on enlisting crews. It usually involved the agents and men in long, expensive legal proceedings which interrupted the business of earning a living. It was not only difficult for the Confederates to obtain crewmen who would serve on the cruisers but also it was nearly impossible to find recruiting agents.⁴⁴

In addition to these direct methods of preventing the *Florida* from engaging a new crew, the United States did not remain silent on the diplomatic front. Dayton protested to the French foreign minister that the Confederacy had no right to claim "dire need" since she had voluntarily discharged many men. He insisted that the French action in this case amounted to increasing the armament of the ship, and was, therefore, a violation of neutrality.⁴⁵ Although this protest was rejected, it served to embarrass the French.

These difficulties forced the *Florida* to ship men of all nationalities, a situation which led to numerous problems. The Spanish and Italian seamen did not get along well with the English and American crew members. Many of the recruits were unfamiliar with the ship, her machinery and often with the English language. Eventually, the Confederacy obtained enough crewmen to operate the ship, but not as many as were needed.⁴⁶

Maffitt's replacement, Commander J. N. Barney, who took charge in September and supervised most of the repairs made on the ship, became ill with chronic dyspepsia and was also forced to request that he be relieved from command. Barney was the same man who was to have replaced Maffitt at Mobile, but once again he was unable to take the ship to sea. According to Surgeon Charlton, Barney's illness was caused by the diet and confinement of life on shipboard, and only fresh food and exercise would cure him. In any case, Barney was unfit for a long cruise." He was relieved from command of the *Florida* on January 9, 1864, by Lieutenant Charles Manigault Morris." And so it was that the *Florida,* with trials and tribulations enough already, had three commanders while she was at Brest.

The new commander was a native of South Carolina. He had resigned from the United States Navy on January 29, 1861, and had joined the Confederate Navy. He commanded the gunboat *Huntress* at Savannah for a time and later did ordnance duty and commanded the naval rendezvous there. Early in 1863, he was ordered to Europe for duty on one of the new Laird Rams, but when these ships were seized, he was given command of the *Florida.*" Morris showed himself to be an experienced and competent officer, but he lacked the dash and imagination of Maffitt.

Upon assuming command in January, Morris took the ship on a trial run around the harbor, and he was disappointed to discover that, in spite of the extensive work, she still needed additional repairs. With energy characteristic of a new commander, Morris immediately set about completing the necessary tasks." The job was at last finished on February 9, and although much time and money had been spent, Morris was not entirely satisfied with the ship's performance. He believed the decreased efficiency was a consequence of the fact that French workmen had been unfamiliar with the

Florida's machinery and that this had resulted in work of a poor quality.

Despite all his efforts Morris had been unable to obtain a full crew for the ship, as has been noted. He was still short-handed to the extent that he would not be able to man all his guns. Because of this paucity of crew members, he planned to have one of his seven-inch guns pivoted to each side and use one crew for both guns. The pivot guns were almost useless on their present carriages and were actually less efficient than the light broadside battery. Morris reported that he did not intend to send a list of his crew until he was out of port since he had a number of "servants" on board who would not sign on as crew members until the ship was at sea.[51] This practice of carrying men to sea as "servants" or "passengers" was used to circumvent neutrality laws. The French government could truthfully say that the *Florida* had not enlisted these men for duty while in France's waters, thus avoiding complications with the United States.

A new commander plus a new crew must certainly have added to the problems of running the ship. Fortunately, several of the junior officers, including the executive officer Lieutenant Averett, who had been on board since she left Mobile, were still on the *Florida* and able to advise Morris.[52] The record of the ship's second cruise shows clearly that the problems of an inexperienced crew and a new commander were great and had the effect of reducing efficiency.

Another tactic resorted to by the United States in her effort to stop the *Florida* was to dispatch a warship to watch her. On September 17, the Federal ship *Kearsarge* put into the harbor at Brest.[53] Captain Winslow of the *Kearsarge* apparently hoped to catch the *Florida* as she left that port, but upon his arrival, he was informed by the French authorities that according to the established rule, two vessels of different belligerent powers could not leave port together. One must preceed the other by at least twenty-four hours, thus preventing immediate pursuit.[54]

Winslow remained at Brest from September 17 until October 31, watching the *Florida* and carefully noting her activities. On September 22, the day the Confederate ship was hauled out of dry dock, he called his crew to general quarters, but when it became obvious that the enemy was not preparing to leave the yard, the waiting and watching was resumed.[55] When the cruiser was moved to another anchorage, the *Kearsarge* again got up steam and cleared the ship for action.[56] During the next few days there was considerable activity on board the *Florida,* consisting of cleaning the ship with a large force of mechanics and carpenters.[57] This activity apparently attracted Winslow's attention and once again he got up steam and for two days kept the crew alerted and ready for action.[58]

Winslow reported in a letter to Dayton that at this time he planned to ignore the twenty-four hour rule and try to intercept the *Florida* if she attempted to run out of Brest. He indicated that he believed the only way for him to apprehend the ship would be to chase her out of the port, since he could not hope to blockade the entire area with the *Kearsarge* alone. There were three channels leading to the open sea, and at least two more warships would be needed to cover all the channels and have any chance of capturing the enemy vessel.[59] Apparently, Winslow or the United States Consul at Brest had been able to find out the state of repairs on board the *Florida.* He reported that the Confederate ship would not be ready for service before the end of October and he also discovered that the ship did not have her full crew and was desperately trying to recruit.[60]

Winslow believed it would be worthwhile to challenge

the *Florida* to a fight, and on October 9, he sent a message to the Confederate ship, offering to fight her whenever she left port.[61] The *Florida* wisely refused to accept the challenge. Evidently, some Federal officials believed the challenge had not been considered real, and a stronger, more definite one might get results. Edwin G. Eastman, United States Consul at Queenstown, Ireland, and a former sea captain, suggested that Winslow send a letter to the captain of the *Florida*, explaining the tonnage and weight of metal of his ship and again challenge the Confederate vessel. Eastman believed the two ships were of about equal strength, but Captain Winslow thought the *Florida* was a much weaker ship and, therefore, justified in refusing to fight. Eastman pointed out that although on paper the *Florida* seemed to be stronger, he doubted that she could actually defeat the *Kearsarge* because of the superior crew of the Union ship. He wanted this call to combat to be made publicly and actually thought the *Florida* might accept. In any case, such a challenge could do no harm. If she should refuse, many people in Europe would accuse the Confederate captain of cowardice, which would certainly not aid the cause of the South. Eastman thought that because of this risk of honor, the *Florida* could not do otherwise than accept the challenge and he hoped to arouse public interest and thus apply pressure on the Confederates.[62] Even though the *Florida* refused the action, it is significant to note that this was the method used by Winslow to persuade the *Alabama* to fight the *Kearsarge* a few months later.

Winslow's request for more ships to blockade the *Florida* at Brest was denied by Gideon Welles, who felt such a blockade would require the services of several fast, powerful steamers for a long time, and the United States could not spare the ships. Even if this was not the case, Welles thought a blockade would be violently opposed in Europe, and the ships might not be allowed to take on coal in European ports, or such action might even provoke a war with France, which the United States could ill afford.[63]

Winslow's practice of getting up steam every time movement was observed on board the *Florida* was noted by the French, who assumed correctly that he was planning to ignore their twenty-four hour rule. This action led to a strong protest from the French government and a threat to use force if necessary to prevent a violation of the regulation.[64] Whether by coincidence or design, the day before the French protest was delivered the French ironclad fleet put into port at Brest, an action which impressed Winslow immensely. In fact, he described the ironclad fleet as one of the most powerful naval forces he had ever seen. Simultaneously with the arrival of the protest, Winslow received the news that the *Florida* would not be ready for sea for another month or two.[65] He made no more threatening moves in the direction of the *Florida,* and on October 31, the *Kearsarge* put to sea.

By no means did this end the cat-and-mouse game between the *Kearsarge* and the *Florida.* Winslow merely went to Queenstown, Ireland, and after taking on coal, cruised the sea for a few days and then returned to the vicinity of Brest on November 7. He took up a cruising station near the entrance to the harbor. The reason for his hasty departure from Brest was that he had received reports that the cruiser *Georgia* had been sighted in the area, and he hoped to catch this raider at sea, but after a few days he learned the ship had entered the port of Cherbourg. In the report of his activities, Winslow again told Welles that he had little chance of preventing the escape of the *Florida* from Brest because of the harbor's three entrances. However, he believed his best station would still be at Brest, since the *Georgia* was being watched and he would be notified immediately if she left. Since the *Kearsarge* and the *Georgia* were not in the same port, France's twenty-four hour rule would not apply. Winslow believed for this reason that he would have a better chance to catch the *Georgia* while at the same time he could continue to watch the *Florida*.⁵⁵

The *Kearsarge* remained at Brest during the rest of November and until December 5, when she put to sea again. The log of the ship mentioned, however, that on November 18, a French warship anchored nearby indicating that the Federal vessel was being closely watched.⁵⁷ This vessel was the French ship of the line *Louis XIV*, which had been ordered to keep a close surveillance on the *Kearsarge* and make sure she did not violate French neutrality.⁵⁸ This action apparently caused Winslow to abandon once and for all the idea of chasing the *Florida* out of Brest. Nevertheless, he did keep up steam much of the time because he did not want to miss an opportunity of catching the *Georgia* if she should put to sea.⁵⁹ He also received information that the *Rappahannock*, the old British warship *Victor* converted into a Confederate raider, had got to sea and run into the port of Calais, thus giving him another ship to watch.⁷⁰

Winslow put to sea on December 5, and cruised near the entrance of Brest, which he apparently thought would be the best location from which an interception of any of the cruisers might be made.⁷¹ He maintained this station, with the exception of three trips into the harbor for supplies and a close look at the *Florida*, until January 23, 1864, when he headed for Cadiz, Spain.⁷² The obvious disadvantage of one ship's trying to intercept the *Florida* by cruising off Brest was that sooner or later she would be forced to put into port for supplies and repairs. This, of course, is exactly what happened, and while the *Kearsarge* was making repairs and taking on supplies at Cadiz, the *Florida* quietly slipped out of port and was once more at sea on her second cruise."

The *Florida* was not heard from for some time after that, and for a while it was believed she was planning to join forces with the *Georgia* and *Rappahannock* to attack the *Kearsarge*. While there was no truth to this rumor, the diplomatic officials in Europe were very much concerned over the possibility of such an event."

Chapter Six

The Second Cruise

ON FEBRUARY 10, 1864, after a stay of over five months in the port of Brest, France, the *Florida* put to sea on her second cruise.[1] Upon leaving the harbor, the ship ran into heavy weather, and Morris had an opportunity to observe the handling qualities of his vessel. He reported that the *Florida* was an exceptionally well built ship, but he was most unhappy with her steaming qualities. She could not make more than eight knots under steam alone, which was considerably less than she had made on her first cruise when she had often recorded speeds of more than ten knots while using only engines. This difficulty undoubtedly explains Morris' dissatisfaction with the ship's recent overhaul, but he hoped to be able to improve her speed.[2] He believed one reason for the reduced efficiency was the lack of experienced firemen and engine room crews, a situation which would correct itself as the cruise continued.

The plight of a ship staffed by unskilled firemen was well demonstrated by an incident which occurred on the seventh day out of Brest when an accident happened in the after boiler, reducing both the speed and efficiency of the ship.

This calamity was the direct result of negligence by Fireman Stidel. He opened the lower blow cock on the boiler, went on deck, and forgot to return to close the cock. This allowed all the water to run out of the boiler which became over-heated and burned.[3] Fortunately, Chief Engineer Charles W. Quinn discovered the mishap in time to save the boiler from complete ruin, but damage from the heat was such that the arch of the starboard furnace bulged out nearly three inches and the ends of twenty-six tubes in the smoke box were burned. Five of these tubes were so badly burned that they had to be plugged, and eight more needed to be replaced. This accident, along with the heavy sea, caused the ship to use a large amount of coal.[4]

On February 19, the *Florida* met a steam tug at Belle Isle, an island off the coast of France near the ports of Lorient and Nantes. This same island was used again by the Confederates later in the war when they took over the *Stonewall*, a French-built ironclad purchased from Denmark and com-missioned by the Confederacy in 1865. The tug carried the contraband supplies for the *Florida* which could not be taken on board at Brest, including gun shackles and new carriages and slides for the pivot guns.[5] Apparently, this new equip-ment made the pivot guns usable and solved some of the problems about which Morris had been discontented.

The sudden departure of the *Florida* from Brest left the Federal Navy and diplomatic observers in a state of con-fusion. As has been noted, she had slipped away while the *Kearsarge* was at Cadiz, Spain. Furthermore, her course and destination were a mystery. Captain Winslow had assumed the *Florida* would undergo more extensive repairs, but when he returned to Brest, the raider had already gone.[6] The Union ship then spent the entire month cruising in the English Channel searching for the *Florida*, which was reported in that area.' In fact, during all of February, Federal commanders searched European waters for the Confederate raider. Many ships announced that they had seen the *Florida*, but most of these reports were incorrect. Some came from the Mediterranean, others from the North Atlantic, and some even stated they had seen the elusive ship off the coast of Africa, but none of the reports proved to be accurate. The United States Navy, nevertheless, tried to prove the truth of each statement, and ships were deployed to many of these areas. Considering that the practice of circulating false reports has been used in war since the beginning of recorded history, it is probable that the Confederates themselves or their sympathizers may well have spread some of the rumors.

One such story concerning the sighting of a strange steamer reached the ear of George Preble, who happened to have his ship, the *St. Louis*, in port at Lisbon, Portugal. Preble, the same man who had already had an unfortunate experience with the *Florida* at Mobile, immediately put to sea in pursuit of the suspected ship.' On February 22, he arrived at Funchal Roads on the Portuguese island of Madeira; five days later, on the twenty-seventh, the *Florida* also arrived at Funchal. According to Preble, the raider had on board 117 men and much extra equipment and spare parts for her engines. His statement that the ship carried extra equipment was correct; however, Morris' correspondence would indicate that his crew numbered less than 117 at that time.

Preble tried to persuade the Governor of Funchal to refuse the *Florida* any coal or provisions and reported that the Governor had promised him the Confederate vessel would not be allowed to obtain any supplies. Preble had been very anxious to fight the *Florida*, but because the *St. Louis* was a sailing ship, he had little chance of overtaking this enemy at sea. He wrote Welles that he had no plan to attack the

Florida in port, since this would have been a violation of Portuguese neutrality.[9]

In a later report, Preble stated that the *Florida* had been allowed to take on supplies and twenty tons of coal at Funchal in spite of the Governor's promise. The Federal commander stated that his men were so anxious to fight the Confederate ship that he had felt it necessary to withdraw all shot from his guns to make sure there were no incidents.[10] Gideon Welles later reprimanded him for unloading his guns, for to his way of thinking, Preble had endangered his ship by this action in the face of the enemy.[11] According to Preble's information, Morris had said he had no intention of fighting the *St. Louis* unless he could get her in a calm where the *Florida's* steam engine would give the Confederates the advantage. Morris believed he could ill afford any damage to his ship, since repairs were too difficult and time consuming to make.[12]

After leaving Belle Isle, the *Florida* had continued southward, experiencing nothing unusual until she reached Funchal on February 27. During this entire trip, she had seen only two ships and one of these, the *George Channing*, was bound to New Zealand and, therefore, would have been unlikely to have reported the location of the *Florida*.[13] This infrequency of contacts no doubt explains why no one really knew the ship's location until Preble met her at Funchal.

After he arrived at Funchal, Morris was ordered by the Governor to leave immediately, whereupon Morris answered that he could not leave until he had coal, bread, and water, since to do so without these necessities would endanger the ship. Morris reminded the Governor that the aid which he was requesting was identical to that which the English, French, Brazilian, and Madeira's own Portuguese governments had granted in the past.[14] In answer to this letter,

Governor Castelbrance informed Morris that he could have bread, water, and twenty tons of coal, but that he would have to leave port within twenty-four hours.[15] Morris, hoping to obtain more than twenty tons of coal, sent another message to the Governor in which he said that this amount of coal would not be sufficient to run the ship safely, and he insisted that he would not leave port until he was granted at least forty tons.[16] The Confederate commander followed this message with a personal call on the Governor at which time Castelbrance told him that unless the *Florida* left port that evening, she would not be allowed to take any coal at all. With little choice left to him, Morris agreed to take the coal and leave port. He reminded the Governor that the treatment accorded the *Florida* was not fair, since the Federal ships were allowed to take all the coal they wished. Morris was convinced that the action of United States Consul Robert Bayman was responsible for the *Florida's* misadventure at Funchal.[17]

This inability to obtain sufficient coal and other supplies was typical of the hardships suffered by the Confederate raiders at the hands of the diplomatic officials of the United States. This incident alone, which involved only a small amount of coal, was protested vehemently not only by Consul Bayman but also by James E. Harvey, United States Minister to Portugal.[18] Because of this constant barrage of protests by the diplomats of the United States, the Portuguese and other governments preferred to avoid any intercourse with the Confederates. Regardless of the right or wrong involved, these protests were always annoying to the governments receiving them, and there can be no question that this action hampered the operations of the raiders.

Upon leaving the port of Funchal, the *Florida* sailed for the island of Tenerife, where it was believed she could complete her coaling and take on fresh supplies. Morris experienced no difficulty obtaining necessary provisions there and remained in port only a short time. The morning after the *Florida's* arrival at this port, March 5, 1864, the *St. Louis* was sighted, but since Morris wished to avoid a fight with this ship, he put to sea immediately.[19] Preble, predicting that Morris would go to Tenerife when he left Funchal, followed in hot pursuit still hoping to provoke a fight. Thus, the Governor at Madeira not only refused to allow the Confederate ship to take on adequate supplies, but it was apparent also that he had not enforced the twenty-four hour rule on the Union ship at Funchal. But once more, Preble's attempt was doomed, and because of his lack of a steam ship, the frustrated Federal commander was again forced to watch the *Florida* steam away.[20]

After the *Florida* left Tenerife, she continued her cruise for the next three weeks with no unusual activity aboard. Several ships were sighted, but none proved to be American. Morris used this period of inactivity to train his new crew in the use of heavy guns, to scrape and paint the ship, and to make new carriages for the two pivot guns.[21]

On March 29, the *Florida* captured the ship *Avon* of Boston, bound from Howlands Island with a cargo of 1600 tons of guano. The *Avon* was stripped of valuables and then used for target practice. Following a custom frequently used by the Confederate cruisers, Morris persuaded twelve of the *Avon's* crew to enlist on his ship. On April 4, Morris overhauled the bark *Francis Milly* of London and persuaded her captain to take on board the *Avon's* captain, his family, and three crew members, thus ridding the *Florida* of most of her prisoners. However, it was necessary to transfer a large amount of bread and other supplies to the British ship in order to feed the new passengers. Three days later the remainder of the prisoners were placed on board the Spanish ship *Margerita,* bound for Cadiz. During the next two weeks the *Florida* stopped and boarded a number of ships, but none proved to be American. The crew was again kept busy with gun drills and making repairs. On April 26, the ship anchored in the port of Saint-Pierre, Martinique.[22]

From the time the *Florida* left Tenerife until she arrived in Martinique, the United States Navy was besieged with reports that she had been sighted in all parts of the world. F. H. Morse, United States Consul at London, reported on March 4, that the *Florida* was believed to have gone to the Mediterranean.[23] The London *Times* stated on April 15th that the cruiser had recently been in port at Bermuda.[24] The importance of these reports, when viewed in context, was that they showed that whenever the *Florida* was at sea, the Federal government had no idea of her location, and because of its tremendous desire to capture or sink the raider, most of these reports had to be investigated. Federal cruisers were, therefore, dispatched to the seven seas.

The *Florida* remained at Saint-Pierre for five days, during which time coal and provisions were taken on board, and half the crew was given liberty. It was necessary to give some shore leave to the crew in order to maintain morale, but this practice nearly always lead to a number of desertions, and of the men allowed this privilege at Saint-Pierre, six failed to return.[25] Except that these losses sometimes left the ship shorthanded, they frequently eliminated the most undesirable part of the crew at no cost to the Confederacy since their wages were not paid.

While in Martinique, Morris was forced to relieve two of his officers because of illness. Lieutenant James L. Hoole, one of those considered too ill for additional sea duty, was afflcted with a serious lung disorder, and since he had been on the sick list for nearly four months without improvement, Surgeon Charlton recommended he be sent home.[26] Morris commended Hoole as a good officer and asked that he be reassigned to the *Florida* in the event his health improved.[27] Hoole returned to the Confederacy where his health did improve to some extent but he was never able to go to sea again. Eventually, he joined the army as an artillery officer where he fought until the end of the conflict. He died shortly after the war of tuberculosis, undoubtedly the disease which ended his career at sea.[28]

In addition to the loss of Lieutenant Hoole, Morris accepted the resignation of Second Assistant Engineer J. C. Lake, who was also very ill.[29] According to Dr. Charlton, Lake was totally unfit for duty since he was afflicted with secondary syphillis.[30]

The visit of the *Florida* at Martinique was eventually reported to the American cruisers in the area, and Admiral James L. Lardner, Commander of the West Indian Squadron, spent most of the month of May cruising around St. Thomas and Martinique in his flagship, the *Powhatan*, in a fruitless search for the *Florida*. Lardner's anxiety was increased by the fact that the California steamer was due to be in those waters.[31] The California steamers were fast ships which carried gold from the mines in California to the East Coast of the United States, and because of their speed these vessels usually ran without convoy. One steamer would carry its load of gold, passengers and valuable merchandise from California to Panama where all passengers and goods were transferred to a railroad, taken across Panama and loaded on another steamer which completed the trip to the East Coast. The steamers used on both legs of this journey were referred to as California steamers, and since they carried large amounts of gold, there was always great fear that one of them would fall into the hands of a Confederate raider.

The reports of the *Florida's* location caused Gideon Welles to order the steamer *Iroquois* to reinforce the United States' strength in the West Indies. Welles said that if the *Florida* seemed to have left the West Indies, the *Iroquois* was to proceed down the coast of Brazil and from there to the Cape of Good Hope, where she was to cruise until ordered elsewhere.[32]

While Lardner was searching for the *Florida* around St. Thomas, the Confederate ship had, upon leaving Martinique, set a course in the direction of Bermuda. Nothing unusual happened to the raider while she continued to stop and board ships, none of which was American. On May 12, the *Florida* neared Bermuda where she exchanged salutes with Her British Majesty's gunboat *Nimble*. This incident was somewhat unusual since Britain did not recognize the Confederacy. Apparently word of this event failed to reach the Federal authorities since there was no protest and there most certainly would have been, had the United States learned of this action.

Morris considered it necessary to send dispatches to the Confederacy at this time, and he chose Lieutenant S. W. Averett to carry the messages. Averett was selected at the suggestion of Dr. Charlton because he was suffering from chronic vertigo believed to have been caused by overwork.[33] Morris' urgent need to communicate with the Confederacy came as a result of the condition of his personnel. It was necessary to have immediately a new staff of engineers and replacements for Hoole and Averett before the ship would be safe. Certainly, no coastal raid on the United States or any other extensive action could be carried out until such replacements were made. The most critical problem was in the engineering department where Second Assistant Engineer Lake had been discharged and Acting Chief Engineer Quinn was frequently ill.[34] Dr. Charlton reported that Quinn had had attacks of nephritic colic on an average of about twice a month for the previous six months.[35] D. McWilliams, the First Assistant Engineer, constantly complained of ill health and was not considered dependable. In fact, the only engineer whom Morris considered dependable was Walter Rose. Because of such a limited staff, Morris reported to Mallory that he could use the ship's engines during only one watch. He also stated that because the *Florida* had taken so few prizes, she had been forced to operate with less funds than he thought desirable. It had been necessary to spend entirely too much on supplies and coal, and the ship was actually short of money. Morris asked that funds and men be ready for him at Bermuda about June 12, 1864, when he would return to that port.[36]

Along with this message to Mallory, Morris included the report of Chief Engineer Quinn concerning the condition of the engineering department. Quinn confirmed his commander's evaluation of the situation, adding that the engineers were dissatisfied, and Rose, the one engineer Morris said was dependable, wanted to leave the ship as soon as he could. One of the most perplexing situations was the seeming inability to get competent water tenders and firemen who knew their work or could be trusted. Quinn said the engineers had to move continuously between the fire rooms and the engine room to make sure these men were performing assigned tasks and the boilers had water in them. He believed this was the reason for the ship's ever constant tribulations with her machinery and boilers, and unless changes were made, the *Florida* would continue to have accidents and not get full efficiency.[37] This situation would explain why the ship had suffered from almost constant engine trouble, especially since she left Brest, and would certainly preclude a raid on the coast of the United States.

After putting Lieutenant Averett ashore at Bermuda, the *Florida* continued her cruise without incident until May 18, when she captured the schooner *George Latimer* of Baltimore, carrying a cargo of bread, flour, and lard, and bound for Pernambuco, Brazil. After bringing the officers and crew aboard the *Florida*, Morris stripped the prize of valuable supplies and burned her. The cargo of this ship proved to be extremely useful to the Confederates since these supplies enabled them to remain at sea for a longer time. During the days following the capture of the *Latimer*, there was no unusual activity aboard the raider. Three members of the prize's crew were signed on board the *Florida*, and on June 5, the remaining prisoners were put aboard the British ship *Nourmahal*. After this transfer of prisoners, the *Florida* continued to cruise, stopping several ships, none of which was American, until June 17, when she captured the *W. C. Clarke* of Boston. The captain of the *Clarke* protested bitterly to Morris, stating that the cargo of his brig belonged to Spanish merchants and, therefore, should not be destroyed. Morris was not accustomed to demolishing neutral cargoes, but in this case, the captain had no proof of the cargo's neutrality, and in the end Morris burned the ship.[35]

Since it was generally known that the Confederate raiders would not destroy neutral cargoes, nearly all United States ships carrying such goods had papers to prove conclusively the ownership. It was, in fact, a common dodge of American merchant men to obtain fraudulent papers to try to protect themselves from the raiders. Because these practices were well known, Morris had every reason to expect any ship carrying neutral cargo to have the necessary proof.

On June 18, the *Florida* arrived in the port of St. Georges,
Bermuda, where all prisoners were released.[39] Upon his
arrival there, Morris was presented with a communication
from Vice Admiral James Hope of the British Navy which
protested the burning of the *Martaban* by the *Alabama*. The
Admiral pointed out that the ship had carried legal British
papers, and while being of doubtful character, she should
not have been burned. Hope agreed that a belligerent had
a right to burn an enemy ship at sea but felt it had no right
to destroy a ship if there was any uncertainty as to her
character. The Admiral reminded Morris that if there were
any possibility of a ship's being neutral, she should be sent
to an admiralty court for adjudication. He indicated that he
had ordered the officers under his command to capture any
ship which was found guilty of burning British vessels and
to send any ship captured under such conditions to England
for a trial before an admiralty court.[40] This was a good
example of the problems faced by the Confederacy. It was
impossible to send prizes to admiralty courts within the
Confederacy, and because of this, ships which appeared to
have legal papers were allowed to pass unharmed. There
were any number of United States flag ships which had
changed their registry to foreign governments to protect
themselves. The *Martaban* was probably such a ship, and
apparently Captain Semmes of the *Alabama* believed these
papers were forged as this was also a common practice.
Morris replied to Admiral Hope's protest that he had always
allowed all neutral vessels to pass unharmed, and his government had instructed him to take such action.[41] Apparently,
this answer was satisfactory since Morris received no
additional communications on the subject.

While at Bermuda, Morris requested permission to purchase coal and provisions and to repair the ship's propeller,

the after boiler, and one of the valves, which was below the water line. He asked that he be allowed to have this work done at the government dock yard at Inland Island.[42] The extent of the damage to the ship was reported by Chief Engineer Quinn, who said the propeller had developed an injurious shake and jerk which he believed was caused by the fact that the outboard crutch was loose or sprung. Quinn also said the kingston blow valve to the after boiler had been carried away in some sort of accident, and because it was below the water line, he could not repair it. Also, the ship was unable to make full speed because of leaks in a number of the tubes.[43]

As a result of this request for assistance, the *Florida's* machinery was inspected by a group of British naval engineers.[44] They determined the damage could be repaired in about five days, and the cruiser was given five working days to accomplish this.[45] The next few days were used in getting the ship into good condition for cruising as well as for taking on large amounts of provisions, cleaning the bunkers of coal dust, and refilling them with a full supply of good fuel. Since permission had not been granted to use the government dockyard, divers made the repairs on the valve and propeller and scraped the ship's bottom, adding considerably to her speed.

When Morris reached Bermuda, he found Lieutenant Thomas K. Porter and First Assistant Engineer William Ahern waiting to join the *Florida.*[46] Chief Engineer W. S. Thompson and Second Assistant Engineer John B. Brown, two additional replacements which had been requested, arrived on June 26, and reported on board the ship. Upon the arrival of these men, Morris accepted the resignations of his entire engineering department except the ailing Quinn, who was ordered to return to the Confederacy.[47] The fourth replacement, Second Assistant Engineer Charles H. Collier, did not arrive while the *Florida* was in port, and Morris was forced to continue his cruise without him.[48]

As he had requested, Morris also received some additional funds while in Bermuda. The money was in the form of a sight draft for $50,000 on the account of Captain J. D. Bulloch in care of Fraser, Trenholm and Company, Liverpool.[49] Morris was, however, able to obtain only about $42,000 in British gold from the Confederate agent in Bermuda, Major W. S. Walker.[50]

Along with the funds, Morris received a dispatch from Secretary of the Navy Mallory in which Mallory approved of Morris' plan for a coastal raid on the commerce of the United States, but he believed such a raid around the mouth of the Mississippi River would bring about swift pursuit by Union cruisers, and the *Florida* might easily be trapped in the Gulf of Mexico. If Morris wished to make such a raid, Mallory thought he might consider capturing the blockading steamers off St. Marks and Apalachicola. Each of these Florida towns was blockaded by a single small steamer. Mallory believed Morris could capture these steamers and send them to St. Marks under prize crews. He also suggested that Morris might consider making a dash at the New England commerce and fisheries which he thought might be both safer and more profitable. Mallory left to Morris' judgment the ultimate decision as to which, if any, of these raids would be conducted. The Secretary warned him that the United States was now making extensive use of the practice of putting ships under foreign flags for protection. Morris should be especially suspicious of ships operating between the United States and Brazil. A number of these ships were using the Brazilian flag fraudulently. Mallory told the commander to use his own judgment about these vessels but to examine their papers with extreme care.[51]

After Morris left Bermuda, he found that five crew members had deserted. However, they were more than replaced by the enlistment of thirty men, who put to sea in the *Florida* but signed the articles only after leaving the port. One of these who signed on the ship at that time was First Class Fireman James Butler, who had escaped from the United States after having been captured on board the Confederate ironclad *Atlanta.*[52]

On July 1, while cruising near Bermuda, the *Florida* captured the *Harriet Stevens* of New York, a bark found to contain valuable stores which were welcomed aboard the raider. Perhaps the greatest find was two cases containing 312 pounds of opium, valuable for use in hospitals as a sedative and also at that time as an anesthetic while operations were performed. Because of the chronic shortage of medical supplies in the Confederacy, Morris determined to send the opium through the blockade. As soon as the goods were removed from the prize, she was used for target practice and destroyed. The prisoners were placed aboard a Danish ship on the same day. The following day, Morris put back into port at St. Georges and transferred the opium to the steamer *Lillian* bound for the Confederacy. Morris tried to load some coal from a tug boat, but this operation was stopped by the authorities almost immediately.[53]

The continued failure of Engineer Collier to arrive at Bermuda forced the *Florida* to leave that port again without a full complement of engineers, but this situation was remedied on July 3 when Morris stopped the British ship *T. H. A. Pitt* from New York. He discovered that W. H. Jackson, Chief Engineer on the blockade runner *Greyhound* at the time of her capture, was a passenger on the *Pitt*. Upon learning that the *Florida* was short of engineers, Jackson volunteered to serve, whereupon Morris appointed him as Acting Second Assistant Engineer in the Confederate Navy. He believed Jackson, who had been promised a chief's position on a blockade runner, would be a very valuable addition to the ship's crew.[54] Having at last obtained a full crew and complement of officers and a good supply of coal, the *Florida* began a cruise which was to take her into the coastal shipping lanes of the United States. It proved to be one of her most profitable raids.

When it was reported in the United States that the *Florida* had been allowed to repair and resupply at Bermuda, there was a vigorous protest forthcoming immediately. Charles F. Adams told British Foreign Secretary Russell that the British at Bermuda had permitted the Confederate raider to remain in port for nine days, make repairs, and obtain all the coal she desired. Adams reminded the British that warships of the United States had not been allowed so much freedom in British ports, and this action toward the *Florida* was a violation of Britain's own neutrality regulations. This incident, protested the United States' minister, was indicative of British partiality to the Confederates.[55] The United States also complained about the toleration of operations by the *Florida* in waters near the coast of Bermuda since the raider had remained about six miles off shore and boarded all ships which approached the island. Adams reminded the British that they had never allowed United States' ships to stay close to a British port.[56]

The British agreed to investigate the matter and take whatever action might be necessary if a violation of neutrality regulations were found.[57] Although this agreement to investigate on the part of the British may sound like the usual diplomatic evasion to stall and then to forget the issue, it would appear that they did take some sort of action. The treatment of Confederate raiders in British ports was never again as favorable.[58]

On July 7, 1864 the *Florida* stopped the Brazilian ship *Olivia*. This ship was a good example of the practice of United States merchants using a foreign flag for protection against Confederate raiders. The ship was American built and the crew was American but the captain was Brazilian. This ship had been under United States registry until 1861, at which time she was transferred to Brazil, and Morris had little doubt that she was still owned by citizens of the United States, but he could not burn her.

Near the coast of the United States, the *Florida* on July 8 captured the whaling bark *Golconda* of New Bedford, loaded with 1800 barrels of whale oil, and after the raider took some supplies from the prize, she was burned. The prisoners taken from the vessel consisted of the captain, two mates, and seventeen men. During the same night, the *Florida* met a Brazilian ship. In order to protect the secrecy of her location, the cruiser identified herself to the Brazilians as the United States ship *Mohican*. At six o'clock the next morning, she captured the American schooner *Margaret Y. Davis* from Port Royal. Seven prisoners were taken off the prize, after which she was burned. The *Florida* then sighted another vessel which she proceeded to overhaul only to find that she was British. Morris was able to persuade the captain to take six of his prisoners. A little later, at eleven o'clock in the morning, the Confederates sighted a bark being towed by a steamer. As soon as the steamer realized the *Florida* was giving chase, she cast off the tow and stood to the west. The *Florida* chased the steamer for about half an hour, but since she could not gain on her, she returned to the other ship. This prize was the American vessel *Greenland* of

Brunswick, loaded with coal for Pensacola.[59] When the *Florida's* crew first went aboard the new prize, they hoped the raider would be able to obtain some of this coal for her own use. However, Morris' chief engineer said it was anthracite and could not be used in the ship's furnace. The prize was then stripped of some provisions and burned. The steamer which escaped was found to be the tug *America* of Philadelphia.[60] This escape was unfortunate for the *Florida* because the *America,* a fast ship, was able to reach port quickly and warn the Navy of the location of the raider. Morris was thus forced to cut short the coastal cruise by one or two days and doubtless lose several prizes.

On July 10, the *Florida* began one of the busiest twenty-four hours periods of her entire career. At around 3:00 in the morning, she sighted a bark which proved to be the *General Barry* of Thomaston, Maine, carrying 1100 bales of hay bound for Fortress Monroe. The *Barry* was overhauled, her prisoners removed, and then she was burned.[61] Three hours later, at 6:00 a.m., the *Florida* boarded the bark *Zelinda* of Eastport, Maine, but since there was another ship in sight, Morris left a prize crew on board this latest acquisition and set out in pursuit of the other ship, the schooner *Howard* of New York. The *Howard* carried a cargo of fruit belonging to English merchants; as a result, she was bonded for $6,000 and used as a cartel for the *Florida's* sixty-two prisoners.[62] After this operation was completed, the *Zelinda* was drawn alongside the Confederate ship where her provisions were unloaded and she was set on fire. All of this action was completed before ten o'clock in the morning.[63] The reason for the capture of such a large number of American ships at one time was because the *Florida* had reached the coastal shipping lanes about thirty-five miles off the Eastern Shore of Maryland.

Soon after the burning of the *Zelinda*, the *Florida* halted a ship which proved to be the English schooner *Lane* with a load of fruit bound for New York. After leaving the *Lane*, Morris pursued a steamer which was American. She tried to escape, but after the *Florida* had fired three shots across her stern, the steamer surrendered. She was the new propeller steamer *Electric Spark* of Philadelphia, bound from New York to New Orleans with the United States mail, forty-three passengers, a crew of thirty-six, and a very valuable cargo. Lieutenant Stone was sent aboard the steamer with a prize crew and ordered to follow the *Florida*. Since the English schooner *Lane* was still in sight, the *Florida* over-hauled her again and persuaded the captain to take the passengers and crew of the *Electric Spark* to the Delaware breakwater, a distance of about seventy-three miles. Among the prisoners taken on the prize were several Federal officers, who were released but forced to give parole.

When Morris captured the steamer, he hoped to put a prize crew aboard and run her into Wilmington, North Carolina, but he decided against this attempt because he did not have competent men to run the ship. The problem was that he did not have an extra engineer. Second Assistant Engineer Jackson's ankle had just been broken by a falling tackle, and so once more the *Florida* had only three engineers who were able to perform their duties. As a result, Chief Engineer Thompson believed it would endanger the Confederate ship if the force were further reduced. Morris agreed that the loss of another engineer would be too great a risk to take, and so it was decided to sink the prize."

The decision to sink the *Electric Spark* must have been a most difficult one as the prize was a new propeller steamer which had a top speed of twelve knots. The vessel was larger than the *Florida* and could have very easily been converted

C.S.S. *Florida*
(National Archives)

The Original Builder's Model of the C.S.S. *Florida*
(Smithsonian Institution and Maryland Historical Society)

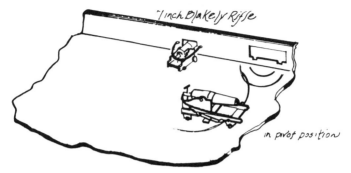

7-inch Blakely Rifle on Pivot Mount and in Broadside
(Drawn by Sally Gould)

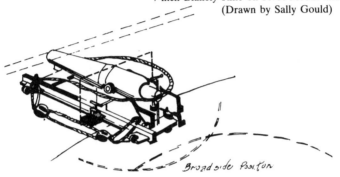

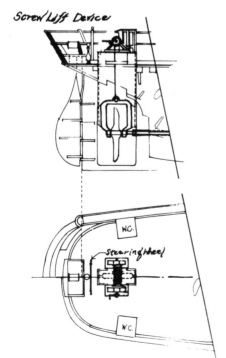

Screw Lift Device
(Drawn by Sally Gould)

John Newland Maffitt—First Captain of the C.S.S. *Florida*
(*Century Magazine*)

C.S.S. *Florida* Running the Blockade at Mobile Bay
(Official U.S. Navy Photograph)

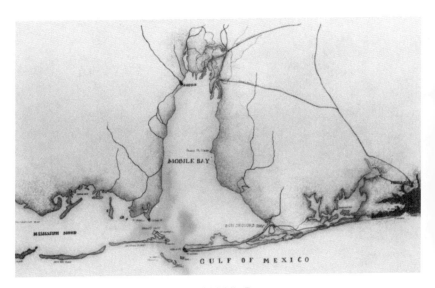

Map of Mobile Bay
(Drawn by Sally Gould)

The *Florida* Destroying the Clipper Ship *Jacob Bell*
(*Harper's Weekly*)

The *Florida* Chasing the Ship *Star of Peace*
(*Century Magazine*)

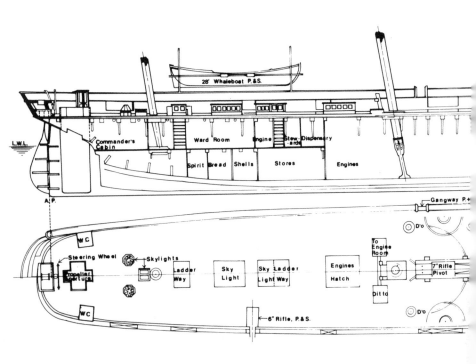

28' Whaleboat P.&S.

L.W.L.

Commander's Cabin

Ward Room

Engine

Stew ards

Dispensary

Spirit Bread

Shells

Stores

Engines

A.P.

Gangway P.+

W C

D'o

Steering Wheel

Skylights

Propeller Aperture

Ladder Way

Sky Light

Sky Light

Ladder Way

Engines Hatch

To Engine Room

7" Rifle Pivot

Ditto

W C

D'o

6" Rifle, P.&S.

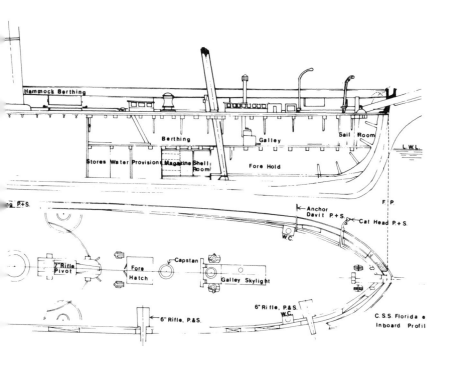

Hammock Berthing

Berthing   Galley   Sail Room

L.W.L.

Stores   Water   Provisions   Magazine   Shell Room   Fore Hold

g P+S.

F.P.

← Anchor Davit P.+S. →← Cat Head P.+S.

W.C.

7"Rifle Pivot

Fore Hatch

←Capstan

Galley Skylight

6" Rifle, P.&S. W.C.

← 6" Rifle, P.&S.

C.S.S. Florida ●
Inboard Profil

C.S.S. *Florida*—Inboard Profile and Deck
(Original drawing by William Geoghegan, Smithsonian Institution,
redrawn for the 1987 edition by Sally Gould)

The *Tacony* Burning Shipping
(*Harper's Weekly*)

Charles M. Morris—Second Captain of the *Florida*
(*Harper's Weekly*)

U.S. Steamer *Vanderbilt*
(National Archives)

The Burning of the Revenue Cutter *Caleb Cushing* by C. W. Read
(*Harper's Weekly*)

Charles W. Read in Midshipman Uniform, C.S.N.
(U.S. Navy Photograph)

The *Florida* and the *Wachusett*
(*Harper's Weekly*)

Napoleon Collins—Captain of the U.S.S. *Wachusett*
(*Harper's Weekly*)

The *Wachusett* Ramming the *Florida*
(*Century Magazine*)

into a cruiser; her draft of nineteen feet was too great for a good blockade runner. The ship, valued at $175,000, carried stores of great worth and would have made a very substantial contribution to the Confederacy. The cargo, composed of assorted merchandise, dry goods, boots and shoes, fine provisions, wines and liquors, was worth between $600,000 and $800,000.[65] Probably a more aggressive commander, such as Maffitt, would have taken the risk and attempted to run the blockade with the prize, even though it would have left the *Florida* short of engineers. It would be hard to say that Morris was wrong in his decision, but certainly he showed himself to be cautious, perhaps too cautious when one considers the value of the prize.

Morris believed that the United States Navy would expect the ship to run the blockade or be made into a cruiser and he thought it would be advantageous to allow this idea to continue. Therefore, instead of burning the prize, Morris had all her pipes cut and air ports opened, permitting the ship to sink and leaving her fate in doubt. He planned to aid his own escape by forcing the Federal cruisers to search for the *Electric Spark* as well as the *Florida*. The prize sank during the night, and at the same time the Confederate ship left the coast of the United States. Morris believed the tug *America* would have reached port, and the enemy would be after him. Before sinking the prize, he removed the mail and Adams Express Company chest. He found no dispatches in the mail bags, but he did find $12,000 worth of postage stamps which he kept, throwing the remaining mail overboard. The Adams Company chest contained $1,305 in United States greenbacks and $219 in gold, $328 in New Orleans bank notes and $132 in New Orleans city notes. The rest of the cargo, valuable though it was, was left aboard the prize.

The capture of the ship was not accomplished without loss

of life to the Confederacy. In the process of removing the prize crew, a boat was swamped and Midshipman William B. Sinclair was drowned when he gave his oar to a crewman who could not swim. For this act of heroism, Sinclair was given a citation posthumously which was read on every ship in the Confederate Navy.[66]

As suspected, the escape of the steam tug *America* meant that the coastal raid of the *Florida* would not go long unnoticed. When the *America* reached port on July 9, all Federal commanders were notified immediately. The news from this vessel was followed by a number of other reports, some accurate and others false, resulting in a state of complete confusion in the Navy Department, which sent all available ships in a fruitless search.[67] Ships explored the entire length of the coast with no success. A good example of the confusion was outlined by Assistant Secretary of the Navy G. V. Fox when he acknowledged that the *Florida* had been reported in four or five different places at the same time.[68] The *Florida*, of course, had long since left the coast of the United States, but the search continued and some cruisers were looking for the ship as late as August 24.[69]

Morris was correct in his assumption that sinking the *Electric Spark* would cause the Federals no end of anxiety.[70] The Navy Department looked on the *Electric Spark* as a source of danger since they believed she had either been outfitted as a cruiser by the *Florida* or else run into Wilmington. No one in the Union Navy seemed to consider the possibility of her real fate.[71]

In addition to the confusion caused the Navy Department by the disappearance of the *Florida*, there was panic along the entire length of the coast. Governor Sam Corey of Maine wrote Gideon Welles and virtually demanded that the Navy provide ships to protect the coast. Corey pointed out that it would be easy for the *Florida* or some other raider to seize the steamers coming out of the Kennebunk River or to make a raid on the unprotected harbors.[12] Corey's demand was doubtless strengthened by some of the false reports which had stated that a strange steamer had been seen off Maine. Apparently, the *Tacony's* raid on Portland the previous year and antics of other raiders had caused considerable apprehension among the people living along the East Coast. When the *Florida* appeared in the shipping lanes near the United States again in 1864, it was only natural that the public should become agitated. The Confederate raider *Tallahassee* also conducted her famous raid during the month of August, 1864. As a result of these activities, the Federal Navy spent the summer hunting the raiders with no success.[13] One wonders what the effect would have been had the Confederacy arranged to have a coastal raid by one or more of the cruisers about every two or three months.

There is little doubt that this coastal raid influenced Gideon Welles to take unusual action in using the services of A. L. Drayton, a prisoner of war who was a former member of the crew of the *Florida* and had been captured on the *Tacony*. Drayton, in offering his services, claimed to have information which would enable the Union cruisers to capture the *Florida*.[14] Welles at length agreed that if the prisoner would provide the United States with correct information, he would be well rewarded.[15] Drayton, playing the part of the informer well, apparently told only a small portion of what he knew at a time, hoping to gain more concessions. In this manner, he stated to Welles that the *Florida* would meet a tender on the twenty-fifth of August at Rocas, about Latitude 3°55′ South, Longitude 33°43′ West.[16] Welles apparently believed Drayton knew where the *Florida* would be, since he had come to Welles' attention by telling his jailer that the *Florida* would make a coastal raid in late June or early July, and when the raid took place, it impressed the officers in charge of the prison enough to let Drayton correspond with Welles. Welles was convinced that Drayton knew the Confederate recognition signal and where the *Florida* would go. In any case, he had the prisoner released."

Drayton, who had only been rated as a seaman on the Confederate ship, passed himself off as having been an officer, and upon his release from prison, he was appointed a pilot in the United States Navy on temporary service and ordered to report to Captain Charles Steedman on board the United States ship *Ticonderoga*. The *Ticonderoga* was to be sent to search for the *Florida,* and the implication was that this Federal warship would go wherever Drayton thought the *Florida* might be located." Just how valuable Drayton would have been to the Federal Navy cannot be known since the *Florida* was captured before the *Ticonderoga* had been at sea more than two months, and Drayton was not mentioned in the records again.

As a seaman on the *Florida* it seems doubtful that Drayton ever had any knowledge of the ship's future activities. He may have known the Confederate recognition signals and was doubtless familiar with the habits of the ship while she was commanded by Maffitt. The *Florida* was now, however, commanded by Morris, and Drayton could have known little about her operations. In any case, his prediction of a coastal raid proved to be accurate, and, apparently, it convinced Welles of his knowledge. There is some question as to whether Drayton was really a traitor or whether he had grown tired of prison and decided to see if he could get out. Perhaps he could take a United States warship on a fruitless cruise around the world, thus neutralizing the ship for a long period of time. Whatever he had intended, this seems to have been the effect of his action, and traitor or not he actually benefitted the Confederacy.

After leaving the coast of the United States, the *Florida* set a course to the East, and on July 11, 1864, after one day at sea, sighted an English ship, the *Matilda B*. Since this vessel was bound for Matamoros, Mexico, she could not report the location of the Confederates. Actually, she was probably carrying supplies to Matamoros for the Confederacy and would not have reported the *Florida's* location had the chance presented itself. Morris sighted another English ship on July 12, but this time the *Florida* identified herself as being an American warship. The raider continued on her eastward course for the next few weeks, meeting very few ships, and of these, none was American and apparently none reported the location of the *Florida* to Federal authorities. The first correct information as to the ship's location was sent to the United States when she arrived at Santa Cruz, Tenerife, in August. It took several weeks for information from Tenerife to reach the States and Washington probably did not know the exact location of the *Florida* until around the first of September. In the meantime, the Confederate ship had simply vanished for six weeks. This disappearing act led to dozens of false reports and fruitless searches.

The *Florida* took on fresh supplies and 148 tons of coal at Santa Cruz without difficulty.[79] Also, while the ship was there Second Assistant Engineer Jackson resigned. He had not recovered from his broken ankle and had been unable to perform his duties since July 10.[80] The raider left Santa Cruz on August 5, and set her course toward the southwest for seventeen days, stopping a number of ships, none of which proved to be American. On August 22, she captured the *Southern Rights* of Richmond, Maine. The cargo of 18,000 sacks of rice belonged to English merchants, and as a result the clipper ship was bonded for $35,000 and allowed to proceed. The *Florida* continued to cruise in search of prizes, but in fifteen days, the raider identified twelve ships, none of which belonged to the United States.[81]

It is apparent that this general scarcity of prizes, the *Southern Rights* being the only ship taken in two months of almost constant cruising, caused considerable boredom and uneasiness aboard the ship. The *Florida* had made only one port of call during this period and gave no shore leave while there. At any rate, on September 11, a note was written to Morris indicating that some members of the crew were near mutiny. This unrest was certainly a result of too much time at sea and not enough to do. The note pointed out that there were several officers who were greatly disliked, and that Lieutenant Porter was the most unpopular of the group.[82] In addition, the Italian, Greek, and Spanish crew members believed they were not receiving treatment equal to that given the Englishmen and Americans, and they resented this and wished to be discharged from the ship.[83]

The discovery of this note led to an immediate investigation and the confinement of several crew members who were soon tried in a court martial on the charge of mutinous conduct. In addition to that group, two other men were charged with sodomy. Both groups were tried on September 20, 1864, and, as a result, eight men were acquitted, two were fined three months pay and given a discharge in disgrace, and one other man was acquitted with the court's recommendation that he be discharged.[84] This was one of the few incidents of serious misconduct aboard the *Florida*. Considering the nature of the offenses, it would seem that the main cause of the trouble lay in the long, uneventful cruise. There is little doubt that this situation caused Morris to believe it was necessary to give his men liberty as soon as possible. Therefore, once in port at Bahia, Brazil, Morris gave shore leave even though there was a United States ship in port. This action was at least partly responsible for the capture of the *Florida.*

During the next two weeks, the *Florida* hailed or boarded nine more ships, but again none was American. On September 26, she captured the *Mandamis* of Baltimore. This bark, sailing in ballast, carried two officers and twelve men. Morris burned the vessel after removing provisions and other valuables. The *Mandamis,* certainly not a valuable prize, was the last ship to be captured by the cruiser. Following the practice of enlisting men from prizes, Morris was able to ship three men from the crew of this vessel. The remaining prisoners were placed aboard the Prussian ship *Klawillen.*[85] After this last capture, nothing significant happened until Morris put into the port of Bahia on October 4, 1864.

The arrival at Bahia ended the second cruise of the *Florida,* during which she captured thirteen prizes, destroying eleven and bonding two. Of the eleven destroyed, six were captured in three days at the time of the raid along the coast of the United States. One of those bonded was also captured at this same time. This paucity of prizes captured during the second cruise can best be explained by the fact that in 1863 there were far more American ships at sea than there were in 1864. As has been mentioned, by 1864 a large number of American ships had been transferred to foreign registry for protection. Morris frequently commented that many of the ships he stopped had formerly been under United States' registry. The proof of this contention can be found in the fact that he stopped almost as many ships as Maffitt, but at the time of Morris' cruise the percentage of American ships at sea was much smaller. It was only when Morris got into the coastal shipping lanes of the United States that he found many American ships. Even these were largely engaged in carrying cargo for the Federal government. While it is true that Maffitt was a more aggressive commander than Morris, it is unlikely that his record of captures would have been much better than that of Morris had he continued with the *Florida* on her second cruise. Morris was cruising in the same area which had given Maffitt his best prizes the year before. However, if Maffitt had commanded the ship on her second cruise, he might have made another coastal raid.

The statistics on ships registered under the United States flag show that there was a steep decline in the number of these vessels during the Civil War.[86] While it is true that American shipping was in a state of decline even before the start of the conflict, there is no question that the Confederate raiders greatly accelerated the process during the war. Not only were many ships transferred to foreign flags, but a large number were laid up in American ports. And the once great American merchant fleet had in three years been reduced to a shadow of its former self, a blow from which the United States' merchant service has never fully recovered during peace time.[87]

Chapter Seven

The Capture of the *Florida*

AT 8:00 ON THE EVENING of October 4, 1864, the *Florida* reached the port of Bahia, Brazil. Unfortunately, as it turned out, the United States steamer *Wachusett,* commanded by Napoleon Collins, had arrived there on September 26 to obtain supplies and was still in port.[1] When Collins saw the strange steamer enter the harbor, he was suspicious of her character and dispatched a small boat to investigate the new arrival.[2] This boat, pretending to be from Her British Majesty's ship *Curlew,* approached the *Florida* and asked her name.[3] When Collins learned the Confederates' identity, he immediately ordered his crew to get up steam and make ready for any action.[4] This preparation was premature since there was no conflict between the two vessels until three days later.

On the morning of October 5, a Brazilian officer came on board the cruiser to inquire as to why she was in the port. Morris told him that the *Florida* had been at sea for sixty-one days and was in need of supplies and repairs. The Brazilian informed him that he would deliver the request to Antonio Joaquim da Silva Gomez, President of the province.

137

Meanwhile, the *Florida* was to have no communication with the shore until an answer was received from the President. At noon, Morris received permission to have an interview with da Silva, who subsequently agreed to allow the Confederate ship to remain in port for forty-eight hours to make the necessary repairs and to obtain provisions. He also agreed to send his chief engineer on board to examine the machinery and determine whether or not more time would be needed.

President da Silva told Morris that he feared there might be some incident or agitation between the *Wachusett* and the *Florida,* implying he was concerned over the possibility that the *Florida* might attack the United States ship. Morris, assuring him that he had no intention of precipitating an action with the *Wachusett* there, stated that his ship would respect Brazilian neutrality and would give Bahia nothing to fear. A Brazilian admiral who was present at the interview suggested moving the *Florida* to a position close to the shore so as to place his country's warships between the enemies, thus reducing the chances of any engagement between them. The President told Morris that Thomas F. Wilson, the United States Consul at Bahia, had pledged that the *Wachusett* would be careful to observe Brazilian neutrality.[5] Wilson later denied having made any such promise concerning the conduct of the *Wachusett.*[6]

Upon his return to his ship, Morris immediately moved the *Florida* to the new location. After an examination by a Brazilian engineer, it was determined that several tubes would have to be removed from the boilers and sent ashore for necessary repairs. The Brazilian believed that the completion of this work would take four days, and agreed that the *Florida* would be allowed to remain in port for that length of time.

When Morris learned that the *Florida* would be permitted

to remain in port and that the United States Consul had promised that the *Wachusett* would respect Brazilian neutrality, he decided to give his crew shore leave. He later explained in his report to Samuel Barron, commander of Confederate naval forces in Europe, that he had every reason to consider the *Florida* safe, and for the sake of his crew's health and welfare, he felt it was proper to give them liberty. Half of the crew were sent ashore on the afternoon of October 5. Upon their return the following day, the remainder of the men and Morris himself went on shore.

Early in the evening of October 5, a boat from the *Wachusett*, carrying the United States Consul, came alongside the *Florida* and attempted to deliver a letter to Morris. After examining the letter, Morris refused to accept it because it was both improperly addressed and did not acknowledge his correct title. The next morning, a Mr. L. de Videky came on board the *Florida* and tried once more to deliver a letter from Consul Wilson. Morris again refused to accept the letter because it was still improperly addressed. De Videky then informed Morris that the dispatch contained a challenge to the Confederate ship to fight the *Wachusett*. Morris replied to de Videky ". . . I would neither seek nor avoid a contest with the *Wachusett*, but should I encounter her outside of Brazilian waters, [I] would use my utmost endeavors to destroy her." With this, de Videky left the *Florida*, and there were no other attempts made by Wilson to communicate with the Confederates.[7]

Upon learning of the entry of the *Florida* into the port of Bahia, Wilson had at once gone on board the *Wachusett* to consult with Collins. According to the Consul's report of this incident, Collins, anxious as he was to capture or demolish the *Florida*, was unwilling to violate international law. After a lengthy discussion of various methods of destroying the ship, they agreed that she would be able to escape if she wished because she was much faster than the *Wachusett*. Wilson thought that the only way to capture the enemy ship would be to attack her in port. Since he could not persuade Collins at this time to take this course of action, he resolved to try to destroy the Confederate vessel himself. The First Lieutenant of the *Wachusett*, L. A. Beardslee; the Paymaster, W. W. Williams; and the Surgeon, M. King, agreed to aid the Consul in the attempt. This group decided to employ a steam tug and run down the *Florida* while she was at anchor. At 2:00 on the morning of October 6, Wilson located a tug available to charter. However, after daylight, when the vessel was examined carefully, she was found to be too small to make the attempt with any guarantee of success. Thus frustrated, the group then sought a larger steamer; this effort also failed because the machinery of the only available larger ship was found to be out of order. Wilson and his fellow conspirators were bitterly disappointed to learn that the *Florida* had been removed to a point between the shore and two Brazilian warships. Therefore, they felt their projected attempt was useless.

On the afternoon of the sixth, Wilson returned to the *Wachusett* again in an effort to persuade Collins to attack the *Florida*. After a prolonged argument, Collins agreed to call a meeting of all the ship's officers in order that their opinions might be heard. All the officers, with the exception of one who was unnamed in the record, agreed that they should try to capture or sink the Confederate vessel immediately. It was after this meeting that Collins made his decision to attack. Wilson did not return ashore as he had volunteered to serve on board the ship. Furthermore, Collins wished no one to leave his ship once the decision to attack had been made. He feared that if a boat were sent to the shore, some member of the crew might tell of the plan, thereby losing the element of surprise. Without this, the whole attempt would be useless.⁸ At 3:00 on the morning of October 7, after careful preparation and with maximum silence, the Federal vessel got underway. Collins steered quietly around the Brazilian warships, which lay at anchor, and directly toward the *Florida,* about five-eighths of one mile away. The *Wachusett,* under full steam, struck the *Florida* on the starboard quarter, cutting down her bulwarks and carrying away her mizzen mast and main yard. After the collision, Collins ordered his ship, which was undamaged, to back away, believing that the Confederate vessel would sink from the blow. While the *Wachusett* was backing clear, she received a few pistol shots from the *Florida* which were returned with a volley of small arms and two broadside guns. Collins stated that the broadside guns were fired against his orders, since he had decreed they would be used only if the *Florida* used her heavy ordnance.⁹

After this volley, the *Wachusett* demanded that the *Florida* surrender immediately or be blown out of the water. According to Lieutenant T. K. Porter, the ship's commander in Morris' absence, the Confederate vessel had only half her crew aboard, and her guns were not loaded; furthermore, he thought the *Wachusett* fully capable of destroying the *Florida* before he could load. Nevertheless, he was unwilling to surrender without consulting some of the other officers. After a brief discussion with Lieutenant S. G. Stone, who also believed resistance to be hopeless, Porter agreed to surrender the ship. He then went on board the *Wachusett* to present his sword and the ship's ensign to Collins, who immediately sent a prize crew to the *Florida.* The Confederate officers were paroled and given the liberty of the ship while the enlisted men were put in double irons, where many of them remained for nearly two months.[10] At the time of the surrender, there were twelve officers and fifty-eight men on board. The remainder of the crew and five officers, including Morris, were on shore.[11]

Since the *Florida* was not in a sinking condition, the crew of the *Wachusett* attached a hawser to her and towed the Confederate ship to sea. This attack had aroused the Brazilian forts and ships, which commenced firing on the *Wachusett* as she moved out to sea with her prize in tow. This firing was ineffective and was not returned by the Federals.[12]

Damage to the *Wachusett* resulting from the action was very minor. Although three men on board the Federal ship were wounded, the injuries of only one proved to be serious.[13] The other losses suffered by the American ship consisted of two boats which were cast adrift. One of these had been used to scout the *Florida* before the attack and was subsequently cast adrift rather than risk attracting attention by the noise of hoisting it aboard. The other, which had been used to carry the prize crew over to the Confederate ship, was lost in the hasty departure from port.[14]

Collins later explained that he had hoped to sink the *Florida* by ramming her, and he blamed his failure on the fact that the *Wachusett* was dragging her anchor during the attack. He reported in a complaint against Lieutenant Beardslee that before the attack Beardslee had been ordered to have the anchor chain unshackled and attached to a piece of larger hawser. This action would have enabled the *Wachusett* to slip her cable without noise. Beardslee reported that the order had been carried out, but when the attack got under way, it was discovered the anchor chain was not unshackled. Although Collins did not say so specifically, he indicated by this explanation that the hawser was to be cut, thus allowing the ship to cast away the anchor chain and move swiftly and quietly toward the enemy. Since the anchor chain was still shackled after the ship was underway, apparently it was difficult either to raise the anchor or cast it loose without considerable noise. This impediment undoubtedly slowed the speed of the ship. Collins also blamed Beardslee for firing the heavy guns of the *Wachusett* against his order.[15] Apparently, nothing was ever done about Collins' charges against Beardslee. There is no record of a Beardslee court martial and he remained in the United States Navy.

Consul Wilson returned to the United States on board the *Wachusett*. He later explained to Seward that he had been unable to leave the ship once the action had taken place.[16] While it was no doubt true that he was unable to leave the ship, it is also very possible that he was afraid to return to Bahia. The citizens of that city were so angry over the unprovoked violation of their neutrality by a warship of the United States that they formed a mob which sacked the United States consular offices and dragged the flag through the streets of the town. Wilson was probably very fortunate not to have fallen into the hands of this mob.[17]

In his report on the capture of the *Florida*, Morris stated that as soon as Lieutenant Porter ordered the surrender, fifteen men jumped overboard in an attempt to swim to shore. Of the fifteen, only six reached safety, and the remainder were shot while in the water. Morris also reported that several men were killed or wounded and one of the officers was seriously wounded. There were seventy-one men and five officers, counting Morris, who were ashore or who escaped from the *Florida*.[18]

Brazilian Commander Gervasio Macebo's report of the capture varied in some details from the other accounts. The differences were probably a result of the fact that the Brazilians observed the action from some distance in the morning twilight. In reporting the incident, Macebo stated that about daybreak on October 7, the United States steamer *Wachusett* was observed leaving her anchorage and approaching the Confederate States steamer *Florida*. When the *Wachusett* passed across the bow of his ship, the Corvette *Dona Januaria,* Macebo hailed the *Wachusett* and ordered that she return to her anchorage immediately. Nevertheless, the Federal ship continued to approach her enemy and commenced firing on her. Apparently, Macebo did not realize that the *Wachusett* had already rammed the *Florida*. When the *Wachusett* failed to come to anchor, Macebo ordered an officer to board her and inform Collins that the Brazilians would fire on him should he attack the *Florida*. The Brazilian officer approached the *Wachusett* in a small boat, hailed her, and delivered the message. Collins answered that he would do nothing else and was about to return to his anchorage. The Brazilians failed to realize the action was over and the *Florida* was already in the hands of the Federals. A short time later, Macebo observed the *Wachusett* moving back toward her anchorage, and for a moment he believed an incident had been averted. However, he soon realized that the Federal ship had the *Florida* in tow and immediately ordered the *Dona Januaria* to open fire on the *Wachusett*. The shots from the Brazilian man of war were ineffective and Macebo ordered the steamer *Paraense* to tow the *Dona Januaria,* a sailing vessel, in pursuit of the *Wachusett* and her prize. The Brazilian ships continued the chase until shortly after 10:00 a.m., when it was apparent that all hope of overtaking the attacker was gone.[19]

Had Morris agreed to fight, the *Florida* might have been the victor for she had certain advantages as a man of war. Not only did the *Florida* have a heavier broadside than the

Wachusett, but all of her guns were rifled whereas only part of the guns on the *Wachusett* were rifled. Because of her rifled battery, the *Florida* would have been able to fight at greater range than the Federal ship. This advantage was increased by the fact that the *Florida* was the faster of the two and doubtless could have maintained whatever range she desired. The *Wachusett* was slightly larger than the *Florida* and would have probably been able to survive greater damage. This advantage of the Union ship would have been greatest had a battle taken place at close range. Morris was aware of the superiority of the *Florida's* rifled battery, and he had stated earlier that if he had to fight, he would do so at long range. Both ships had excellent crews, much practiced in gunnery.[20]

After leaving the port of Bahia, the *Florida* and *Wachusett* sailed in company for twenty-three days, reaching St. Bartholomew, West Indies, on October 29. Upon arriving there, the Wachusett put into port and received provisions, but since the legal status of the *Florida* was doubtful, she was left outside the harbor. During the evening the *Florida* drifted about twenty miles. When the *Wachusett* left port the following morning, she was forced to spend several hours looking for her prize.[21] Collins blamed this delay on Beardslee, who had been ordered to keep the *Florida* in sight of the *Wachusett* at all times.[22] In answer to these charges, Beardslee said that he had never lost sight of the *Wachusett,* but he never explained why he had allowed the *Florida* to drift so far. He also reported that he had been informed that Collins had seriously considered firing on the *Florida* when he found her drifting away. Beardslee reported that if Collins had taken such action, he, Beardslee, would have been "led to the belief that the Confederates aboard the *Wachusett* had captured the vessel" and that his duty to his country would have called upon him to destroy her. He stated that he most certainly would have returned a shell from the *Wachusett* with both broadsides from the *Florida,* which were in readiness, and if he had made a mistake, no one would probably have lived to rectify it.[23] It thus appears that a conflict between the *Florida* and the *Wachusett* was only narrowly avoided while both ships were in the hands of the United States.

The *Kearsarge* was also in port at St. Bartholomew, and Collins transferred the swords and colors of the *Florida* to that ship.[24] He was concerned lest there might be some attempt by the Confederates to take back their ship or the *Wachusett,* and as a result he transferred to the *Kearsarge* Dr. Charlton and eighteen other prisoners.[25] Collins further reduced this risk by allowing eighteen more prisoners to escape at St. Thomas, his next stop after St. Bartholomew where he obtained the coal which was unavailable at the first port.[26]

In his report to Gideon Welles, Collins admitted that he had ordered his executive officer to permit the eighteen prisoners to go ashore in a coal lighter. Once they were on board the lighter, Collins changed his mind and sent two boat loads of armed men after the Confederates, but the prisoners reached shore first, fleeing into the woods. Allowing this escape was an especially serious mistake, since there was a case of smallpox aboard, and the ship was in quarantine.[27] Apparently, Collins' action, which was a violation of Danish law, caused an official protest to be made by the port authorities. The escaped prisoners were eventually rounded up by the Danes and sent to Bermuda. In addition to their protest, the Danes demanded that the United States pay passage for these men to Bermuda, an expense which amounted to a total of around $500.[28]

Upon leaving St. Thomas, the *Wachusett* rejoined the *Florida,* which had been again left outside the port, and the two ships sailed in company reaching Newport News, Virginia, on November 12.²⁹ When they arrived at Hampton Roads, the remaining prisoners were transferred ashore and sent eventually to Fort Warren in Boston. Some efforts were made by Federal officers to persuade the men to take the oath of allegiance to the United States but they had no success. The men were kept in close confinement on poor rations until they were released in January of 1865, at which time they were required to sign a parole to leave the United States within ten days. The men, however, were given no money at the time of their release, and they experienced considerable difficulty obtaining passage out of the country. At length they obtained transportation to England by giving a draft to be paid at Liverpool.³⁰ Welles stated that these men were supposed to have been given twenty dollars each upon their release, but the necessary arrangements were not made in Washington until the first of February, several weeks after the prisoners had been freed.³¹

After the important papers, some guns, and other equipment were removed from the *Florida,* she was placed under the command of Acting Master Jonathan Baker and a small crew. On November 19, while she lay at anchor near Fort Monroe, the *Florida* was involved in a collision with the army transport *Alliance,* which was just getting underway and, therefore, not under good control. The damage done by the *Alliance* was not very serious, but the *Florida's* rate of leakage was increased. Before the accident, water had risen in the bilges at the rate of five inches per hour, but afterward the rate increased to eight inches. In his report, Baker explained that while a leak of eight inches per hour was fairly serious, neither he nor his engineer William

Lannau considered it dangerous. Lannau reported that the leak was under control and that the *Florida's* steam pump could easily keep the ship free of water. Nevertheless, some of the other men aboard who were questioned about the leak considered it more dangerous than either Baker or Lannau; yet under questioning they all admitted that the steam pump had been capable of keeping the ship free of water.[32] All parties agreed that the leak alone was not the cause of the eventual sinking of the *Florida*.

On November 24, Baker was ordered to anchor the ship at Hampton Roads in a position under the guns of the iron-clad *Atlanta*, while at the same time he was cautioned to moor her far enough from the shoals to prevent any danger of her going aground in case the anchor should drag. Baker was told that if he needed any assistance, he should call on the *Atlanta*.[33]

On the morning of November 28, 1864, the *Florida* sank in nine fathoms of water.[34] Because of the intricate diplomatic situation relating to the sinking of the ship, a thorough investigation was held which indicated that the *Florida's* pumps had kept her leak under control until sometime between 10:30 p.m. and midnight on the evening of November 27, when there was a sudden advance in the rate of her leakage. In his testimony before the court of inquiry, Lannau reported that he thought this increased rise in the water was due to the accidental bursting of a sea cock. Lannau believed that the damage was neither a deliberate act nor carelessness on the part of any of his men, since he had known all the men on duty at the time of the sinking for at least six months and thought them to be reliable.

According to James Halkier, the fireman who was on duty when the trouble was discovered, the pump ceased working at a little past 11:00 p.m., and the water rose to the fireroom floor. Halkier then called Lannau, who made some repairs, but the pump still failed to work properly and managed to remove only a small amount of water. When Lannau realized that the ship was sinking, he tried unsuccessfully to start the main engines, but the water soon put out the fires. The deck pumps were manned but it was found that several of them would not operate. The *Atlanta* was signaled, and help was soon sent. Even with extra men aboard, the ship could not be saved.

In questioning Baker, the court of inquiry asked why the ship was not beached to save her from sinking. He testified, as has already been noted, that the main engines would not work, even before the fires were put out and that he was unable to set any sail because the sails had been removed. In any case, the weather was too calm for sails to have been of any use. Baker explained that he could not move the ship because there was no kedge on board, nor was there any other kind of small anchor, and the *Florida* was too far out to run a line to shore. Although there was one cutter on board capable of towing the *Florida,* there were not enough oars available to row the cutter. Not a single tug boat came by from midnight until the next morning after the ship had sunk, a happening which Baker considered strange. Usually an average of one tug per hour had been passing the *Florida*.

The court of inquiry decided that the sinking of the *Florida* was a result of the leak and the failure of the pumps, and these factors were considered to be accidental. Blame for the sinking was not placed on anyone. Despite the findings of the court, there are several factors which were not explained in these hearings. In the first place, it seems strange that the leaking of the ship should increase suddenly, and the steam pump should stop working at the same time, since the pumps had been reported to be operating well an hour before

the difficulties started. Another odd coincidence is that
several of the deck pumps would not function, and this is
especially peculiar in that orders had been given several days
before the sinking to make certain that they were in good
condition. Strange as it may seem, the court never made any
effort to determine why the pumps had not been repaired or
if there was any negligence or failure to carry out the orders
on the part of any of the officers on the *Florida*. If Baker
had thought the *Florida* could be towed by a cutter, why
were the two boats from the *Atlanta* not used? They were
certainly available since they had been sent from the *Atlanta*
and were likely tied up alongside the *Florida* during the
whole operation. In any case, no one raised this question
during the hearing.[35]

According to J. N. Maffitt, Admiral David D. Porter told
him in a conversation some years after the war that he,
Porter, had placed an engineer in charge of the *Florida* with
orders as follows: "Before midnight open the sea cock—
and do not leave that Engine room until the water is up to
your chin—at sunrise that Rebel Craft must be a thing of
the past."[36] It was assumed that Brazil would demand the
return of the ship, and it is certain that whether the sinking
of the *Florida* was accidental or not, the United States government was glad to be rid of the vessel. The attitude of most
officials was well summed up by Admiral Porter, who said,
when the sinking was reported, that it was "better so."[37]

The real position of the United States in the *Florida* case
is clear. Consul Wilson was guilty of complicity. Furthermore, the United States Minister to Brazil, J. Watson Webb,
actually told Collins some time prior to the sinking and in
the presence of four officers of the *Wachusett*, ". . . that he
[Webb] had ordered one or more of the commanders of our
men of war to attack any of the rebel cruisers in any of the

ports of Brazil, or to run them down, or words which conveyed the same meaning, and he [Webb] would make it all right with Brazil."[38] In his report to Seward concerning the matter, Webb regretted that Collins had not been better known to him. He believed that any of the other commanders would have made certain the *Florida* was sunk as soon as she was out of port. In fact, he was much concerned when he discovered Collins had taken the Confederate ship back to the United States.[39]

Webb's plan to capture any Confederate cruiser wherever one could be caught, even in the neutral waters of a Brazilian port, was conceived well over a year before the seizure of the *Florida*. In a letter to Seward in May of 1863, Webb explained that he had explored the attitude of the Brazilian Minister of Foreign Affairs and believed ". . . if we should sink these pirates in Brazilian waters, the government of Brazil would secretly rejoice over the act, and be content with a handsome apology." Webb also said that he had been encouraging United States naval officers in that area to capture Confederate ships wherever possible.[40]

In his reply to Webb, Seward stated that he approved of the negotiations between Webb and the Brazilian Minister of Foreign Affairs. He suggested that more might be accomplished if Webb did not explain in advance exactly what the Union might do. He could properly tell the Brazilians, "If nations shall in violation of our right suffer their ports to become bases for the operations of pirates against us we shall adopt such remedies as the laws of self defense allow. It is the earnest desire of the United States to remain at peace with all nations. We have sought especially to deserve the friendship of Brazil and shall persevere in this friendly policy—so long as the Emperor shall accord to us commercial and national rights, which are not less essential to

Brazil and all other American States than to ourselves."[41] It is also apparent that Seward fully approved of the capture of the *Florida* when he commended Webb for his ". . . fidelity to the national interests which you [Webb] have manifested throughout all your proceedings in the matter referred to [the *Florida* case]."[42]

Public opinion regarding the capture of the *Florida* varied. The press of the United States heartily approved the action; public opinion in Brazil and the Confederacy was outraged; in Europe, the United States was universally condemned. An excellent example of the European attitude concerning this capture can be found in the editorial comments of *Colburn's United Service Magazine,* in the following statement:

"But the daring genius of the Yankee supplies us the something from South America that is news indeed. Everyone knows what tremendous sticklers for 'neutral rights' the United States have ever shown themselves, and they have claimed and obtained compensation from almost every nation under the sun for alleged infractions of them. With such a people surely neutral harbors should be respected. But the chivalrous commander of the 'Wachusett' thinks otherwise; he boards the 'Florida' in the harbor of Rio [Bahia], and carries her off as a prize, and the New York Press applauds the deed as a glorious triumph."[43]

As was to be expected, Brazil, with the backing of world diplomatic opinion, demanded the return of the *Florida.*[44] In his protest to Seward concerning the capture of the *Florida,* the Brazilian charge d'affaires to the United States, Ignacio DeAvellar Barloza da Silva, compared the incident to the capture of the British ship *Grange* in 1793 in the Delaware Bay by the French frigate *L'Embuscade.* This was a violation of the neutrality of the United States, and she demanded that the French government immediately return the ship and liberate all persons found on board the vessel, a demand with which France promptly complied. Barloza further stated that the action of the *Wachusett* was even worse than the *Grange* case because the incident had taken place at night and under circumstances which rendered the *Florida* defenseless. He emphasized that the attack was treacherous, especially since Federal officers had given their word that no such engagement would occur.[45]

Seward, in his reply to this note, refused to admit that the attack was treacherous or that the officers involved had been guilty of prevarication. After a long discourse on the "pirates" *Alabama* and *Florida,* the Secretary claimed that the *Wachusett* had acted without authority and stated the United States government would make amends. While the actions of the *Wachusett* were a violation of Brazilian neutrality, he was surprised that the Brazilians were so outraged, considering the actions of the *Alabama* and the *Florida* which had taken place in Brazilian waters. Seward said the prisoners captured on the ship would be released and allowed to leave the United States, but, of course, the *Florida* could not be returned because she had accidentally sunk at Hampton Roads. He agreed to send a full report of the sinking to the Brazilian authorities as soon as the hearings were completed. Regarding Consul Wilson, since he had admitted helping persuade Collins to make the attack, Seward said he would be dismissed. The Secretary also promised that the President of the United States would suspend Collins and direct him to appear before a court martial.[46]

In addition to Seward's written apology and repudiation of the action, the United States rendered a salute to the Brazilian flag, and Federal officials involved in the case were "punished." On July 23, 1866, the United States ship *Nipsic* fired a twenty-one gun salute to the Brazilian flag at Bahia.[47]

Consul Wilson was dismissed from his post as Seward had promised.⁴⁸ Commander Collins, as agreed, was court martialed for violating the territorial jurisdiction of a neutral government, and was convicted and sentenced to be dismissed from the Navy. His only defense for his action was ". . . that the capture of the Florida was for the Public Good."⁴⁹ After several months, and presumably after Brazilian interest had lessened, Gideon Welles disapproved the sentence and restored Collins to duty.⁵⁰ Interestingly enough, in December of 1862 Collins had captured the blockade runner *Mont Blanc* in British territorial waters near Green Turtle Cay, an uninhabited island of the Bahama group. In this case, Collins had been severely reprimanded by Welles and advised to be much more careful of the rights of neutrals. Collins' defense of his action was that he had been ordered by Admiral Wilkes to ignore the territorial jurisdiction of uninhabited islands.⁵¹ It is a significant comparison to note the difference in Welles' attitude in these two cases. One involved a minor prize taken by violating the territorial waters of a major power while the other was a major prize taken in the port of a minor power.

In all the correspondence between Seward and Barloza, there was no mention of the money which was taken off the *Florida*. According to naval records, the safe had been found to contain $12,600 in American gold, $1,305 in United States legal tender notes, $1,462.25 in Louisiana bank notes, 3,000 pounds in English bills of exchange, and a large sum in United States postage stamps.⁵² It seems strange that Brazil did not demand the return of this money since it was lost with the *Florida*. Although it is possible that the Brazilian government was not aware of the existence of the money, it seems unlikely since the Confederate paymaster, who was not among those captured, made a fairly accurate account of the money in his report to Morris while they were at Bahia.[53] Morris was in communication with the Brazilian government, and it would be surprising if he had not given this information to them. It is quite likely that the *Florida* settlement was allowed to stand because the war ended before the final disposition of the case. There was no Confederacy to which the money could be restored and there was no reason to pursue the issue.

The crew of the *Florida* which had been left at Bahia was sent back to Britain where they were paid off and some were discharged. Since the records were lost, these men were paid off from the paymaster's memory.[54] A number of these men wished to remain in the Confederate service, and Morris was ordered to send any good men who wished to remain in service to the *Rappahannock*.[55] Eventually, Lieutenant Samuel Barron, one of the officers of the *Florida,* and a number of the *Florida's* crew who had been sent on board the *Rappahannock* were ordered to proceed to London where they would be sent to join the crew of the Confederate ram *Stonewall.*[56]

The members of the *Florida's* crew who were captured with the ship were returned to England and paid February 20, 1865. Some thirty of these men who wished to remain in Confederate service were ordered to report on board the *Rappahannock* on March 10, and were sent to join the crew of the *Stonewall* in Spain.[57] Additional men from the *Florida* in Nassau were to be sent to the *Stonewall* when she arrived in that area.[58] These men were no doubt some of those who had escaped from the *Wachusett* at St. Thomas. Thus, it seems that a considerable part of the *Florida's* crew, though not of Southern origin, wished to continue to serve the Confederacy, and by various means they eventually became members of the crew of the *Stonewall.*[59]

Chapter Eight

Conclusion

THE CRUISER "FLORIDA," during her two years of operations against Union commerce, was one of the most profitable military investments made by the Confederacy. While she could not change the outcome of the Civil War, she and her sister ship the *Alabama* appear to have done more damage to the United States in proportion to their cost than any other major activity undertaken by the Confederacy. The *Florida's* experiences were unique, varied, and exciting, and along with the other Confederate cruisers, she damaged the Union cause in a number of different ways. This damage was both physical and psychological as well as immediate and long range, but it could not have been accomplished without the able leadership of tough, resourceful commanders, operating against overwhelming odds. It was the activities of these men which have made the story of the *Florida* an interesting tale of the sea and a useful lesson in warfare and diplomacy.

In spite of the success of the *Florida,* her experiences show clearly the problems faced by the cruisers and the limitations of their operations. Because it was impossible for the *Florida* to supply herself completely from her prizes, it was necessary for her to operate from foreign ports. This situation was complicated by neutrality regulations. These rules forbade the cruiser from increasing her armament and often specified that she could not enter the ports of a particular nation more often than once every ninety days. One of the major difficulties caused by the ninety day rule was the necessity of refitting the British built ship in the French port of Brest. Had she not recently been in a British port at Bermuda, she could probably have been overhauled at Liverpool, where she was built. Workers there were familiar with her machinery, and parts were readily available. If she had been able to use these English facilities, the *Florida* would very likely have been back at sea in one month. As it was, she lost six months of valuable cruising time, and her repairs were not satisfactory. Parts had to be imported, and the French workers were unfamiliar with her machinery.

Another factor complicating the operation of the *Florida* was the activity of the United States consuls and ministers, who used every stratagem and technicality available from diplomatic protests to blacklisting merchants to delay, harass, or prevent the cruiser from obtaining coal or other provisions. These efforts were not usually successful, except in annoying the foreign governments involved. Sometimes, however, the amount of coal was limited and needed repairs were seriously restricted. The limitation on coal, as for example at Funchal, was a most serious problem and made it necessary for the *Florida* to keep a fairly large reserve supply in her bunkers at all times lest she find herself forced to leave port without a new stock. This shortened the safe cruising range of the ship and forced her to spend much valuable time searching for ports in which she could obtain coal. Her only other alternative was to sail aimlessly in an out-of-the way place waiting for the ninety day regulation to expire so she could re-enter a port. It was certainly the fuel problem which delayed coastal raids by both Maffitt and Morris, and had coal been readily available, the *Florida* would have doubtless made more such exploits.

Another major hindrance to the successful completion of the *Florida's* mission was her inability to send her prizes to the Confederacy. This meant that all ships captured had to be burned, or if they carried neutral cargo or more passengers than the *Florida* could accommodate, they had to be bonded. If it had been possible for all the prizes which could not be destroyed at sea to have been condemned in an admiralty court, they would have made a large and needed contribution to the Confederacy's treasury.

Recruiting men for the *Florida* was a major problem at all times. Her difficulty at Brest and the necessity of running the blockade at Mobile illustrate this obstacle. Her entry into Mobile Bay made her the only ship built in Britain as a cruiser to commence her operations from a Confederate port. It is doubtful, however, if this distinction was to her advantage. While she forced a large number of Federal ships to watch Mobile and at the same time she recruited a better crew there than she might otherwise have expected, these factors did not compensate for her lost time. She spent five months at Mobile at a time when commerce raiding would have been most profitable.

The *Florida's* cruise illustrates the fact that the commanders more than any other single element determined the ultimate success of the ship. Under the able, imaginative Maffitt this ship came close to matching the record of Semmes and the *Alabama*. On the other hand, the more cautious Morris had a much less colorful career. It is a well recognized fact that there were fewer United States ships at sea during the period of the *Florida's* second cruise. Nevertheless, it is quite probable that had Maffitt remained in command, he would have taken more prizes than Morris, even if he had had to attempt a whole series of coastal raids. Certainly, there is doubt that Maffitt would have left the *Florida* in a position where she could have been captured so easily as Morris did at Bahia. Morris was not actually negligent, but perhaps Maffitt had a far more suspicious nature. It seems very unlikely that Maffitt would have left his ship in charge of a drunken and sleepy crew just back from shore leave with an enemy ship in port.

In spite of all her dilemmas, the career of the *Florida* demonstrates three important factors: first, the amount of damage that a single ship can do to the commerce of an enemy nation; second, the great difficulty involved in destroying such a raider; and third, the lengths to which the United States was willing to go to eliminate this menace. Guerilla warfare has been described as a series of pin pricks that eventually bleed the enemy to death. Commerce raiding, or *guerre de course,* might be characterized as the guerilla warfare of the sea. In minimizing the importance of the Confederate cruisers in the Civil War, historians have followed the time-worn pattern of placing little emphasis upon the significance of guerilla activity. Perhaps the lack of great battles or vast losses in a single encounter may be responsible for this. It is only when one totals the damage over a long period of time that the real significance appears.

The Confederacy built cruisers in the hope of diverting large numbers of ships from the Union blockade and thus weakening the economic stranglehold on the South. It was also expected that the cruisers would apply economic pressure on the North and thereby weaken both the will and ability of the United States to continue the war.

In the first effort, the hopes of the South were not fully

realized because of the singlemindedness of Gideon Welles, who saw that it would be necessary to maintain the strength of the blockade if the South was to be defeated. In making this decision Welles was forced to ward off the tremendous pressure of an aroused public. The newspapers and miscel· laneous correspondence of the Navy Department are some indication of just how much criticism was leveled at him. In spite of his determination to hold the blockade at all costs, even Welles was compelled to relent to a degree during the coastal raids of the *Florida* and the *Tacony*, and some ships were actually taken off blockade duty and sent after the raiders. If it had not been necessary to send some of her fastest ships in search of the raiders, the Navy could have maintained a stronger blockade. Ships like the *Wachusett*, *Kearsarge*, and *Vanderbilt* would have been useful additions to the squadrons at Wilmington or Mobile, and the success of the numerous blockade runners attests to the fact that the United States was not entirely successful in stopping foreign trade with the South. It has been estimated that the cruisers diverted from other duties United States naval vessels equaling around ten times their own tonnage.[1]

As to the other mission of the cruisers, the destruction of commerce, the degree of success was almost unbelievable. The American flag, which in the 1850's had flown over almost as many merchant ships as the British, was nearly swept from the sea, a blow from which the United States merchant service did not recover until 1918. It has often been noted that the carrying trade of the United States was in a state of decline at the start of the war, and that the war only hastened its ultimate doom. However, it is questionable whether this great fleet might not have made a recovery had it not been for the losses suffered on account of the war. There is, in fact, evidence that surplus foreign vessels plus a general lack of

American shipping led to an overall loss of interest in the American merchant fleet both by investors and by the Federal government.[2]

The direct damage caused by the cruisers has been estimated at between $15,500,000 and $25,000,000, and represented a loss of about 200 ships actually destroyed by the raiders.[3] Of this amount the *Florida* and the ships she outfitted accounted for $4,051,000 worth of commerce as compared with $4,792,000 for the *Alabama* and $2,041,000 for the *Shenandoah*.[4] The *Florida* and her tenders took a total of 60 prizes of which 46 were burned, 13 bonded and 1 recaptured. The *Florida* herself captured 38 of these and her satellites the remainder. The ship cost the Confederacy 45,628 pounds to build and because of her many difficulties she may have cost almost that much more to operate. It would be a fair estimate to say that she cost the South $400,000 to build and operate. This would mean, therefore, that the *Florida* destroyed ships worth ten times her own cost.[5]

The indirect damage caused by the cruisers cannot be estimated accurately because there are entirely too many intangibles. However, the cost to the United States in operating ships to search for the cruisers has been tentatively set at $3,325,000, a figure several times greater than the cost of all the cruisers.[6] Another result of the cruisers' operations was the greater premium on war risk insurance which had to be paid by the ship owners and ran into millions of dollars. It was this increased cost of insurance ranging from four to nine dollars per $100 of insured value which really ruined the shipping business. Interestingly enough, panic on the part of the insurance companies seems to have been a major factor in causing such high rates because actual losses did not run much more than double the usual rate of loss from natural causes. Yet insurance rates on some routes were as much as fifteen times what they had been in the ante-bellum period. This situation was reflected in the very large profits made by many of the insurance companies. Since cargoes could be placed on foreign ships without need for war risk insurance, all these extra costs had to be carried by the ship owner rather than the customer. This costly item eliminated the profit from an already competitive business. The American ship owner, already financially distressed, was also faced with customers who were usually more interested in having their cargoes delivered on time and in good condition than they were in collecting insurance claims months or years later. It was, therefore, natural that these customers would rather place their goods on a foreign vessel in order to guarantee delivery. In order to compete, the American ship owner not only had to pay the cost of insurance but also had to reduce his rates below foreign competition to attract cargo.[7]

The combined effect of all these difficulties was to force the ship owner either to lay up his ship, or find a government contract, or transfer his ship to foreign registry. It was this latter course, followed by many owners, which was a major factor in causing the newest and best American ships engaged in the overseas trade to decline in tonnage from about 2,500,000 tons in 1861 to 1,674,516 by 1864. The coastal trade, which accounted for most of the remaining American total tonnage of 5,539,000 in 1861, also suffered from the actions of the Confederate raiders, but it was not as badly damaged. The ships engaged in this trade, however, were far less valuable as a whole. Most of the coastal vessels were older and smaller than those ships used in the overseas trade. The United States lost its largest, newest, and most valuable ships, "queens of the sea." The loss of these ships undoubtedly caused a decline in that great pride which had once characterized the American merchant service. This loss of pride, while not measurable in a statistical way, may have had much to do with America's turning away from the sea after the Civil War.

An important legal aspect of the transfer of American shipping to foreign flags was that the law forbade the transfer of foreign owned ships to the American flag. Therefore, once a ship was foreign owned, it had to remain so. In this way, the best of American merchant fleet was transferred while much of the remainder was tied up to rot in port.[8]

The operation of the cruisers brought the war home to the North and was another contribution to the war effort of the Confederacy. The loss of ships and the adverse effect on the shipping business hurt individuals and private businesses. The burning of fishing boats by the *Tacony* has been severely criticized as a violation of the rules of war, but this action perhaps more than anything else caused panic and hurt large numbers of the enemy. Certainly, the burning of fishing boats which destroyed the fishermen's livelihood was no worse than burning private dwellings and killing or confiscating the farmers' mules, which were equally his means of earning a living. There is little doubt that the losses to American commerce were a factor in adding to the war weariness of the North, which very nearly elected the Peace Party in 1864.

One aspect of the activities of the cruisers which has generally been overlooked concerned the coastal raids. It is probable that these forays have been neglected because they were not executed by the more widely known raiders. The *Florida* was the only one of the better known cruisers to conduct such excursions. These raids did, however, cause pandemonium along the entire coast and probably produced greater excitement and activity in New England than any other Confederate operation except the Battle of Gettysburg and the St. Albans raid.

It is only when all the damage done by the cruisers is totaled that the real significance of these ships is understood. They could not win the war alone, but they were a factor in the battle of attrition. If the Confederacy had done one-tenth as well in other areas, she would likely have been victorious. Their long range effect was disastrous for the United States merchant fleet, and they were certainly the most successful element of the Confederate Navy.

Notes

1. William H. Seward to Charles F. Adams, Aug., 1861, United States Instructions, Great Britain, Vol. XVII, State Department, Record Group 59, National Archives, Washington, D.C., (hereinafter, Instructions).

2. James D. Bulloch, *Secret Services of the Confederate States in Europe or How the Confederate Cruisers Were Equipped* (New York, 1883), I, 46–54, (hereinafter, Bulloch, *Secret Service*).

3. Bulloch to Stephen R. Mallory, Aug. 13, 1862, *Official Records of the Union and Confederate Navies in the War of the Rebellion* (Washington, 1894–1927), Series II, II, 83–87, (hereinafter, *ORN*).

4. Bulloch, *Secret Service*, I, 56–8.

5. T. Miller to Price Edwards, Feb. 21, 1862, Vol. MCCCXIII, British Foreign Office 5, Public Record Office, London, (hereinafter, FO5).

6. Thomas H. Dudley to Seward, Mar. 5, 1862, United States Consular Despatches, Liverpool, Vol. XX, State Department, Record Group 59, National Archives, Washington, D.C., (hereinafter, C. D.).

7. Copy of Register for Transmission to Chief Register of Shipping, Official Number of Ship 44200. Papers and Letters found in Records Relating to Civil War Claims United States and Great Britain, State Department, Record Group 76, National Archives, Washington, D.C., (hereinafter, Civil War Claims).

8. Bulloch, *Secret Service*, I, 58.

9. *Ibid*, I, 67.

10. Adams to Seward, Oct. 18, 1861, Despatches, United States Legation Britain, Vol. LXXVII, State Department, Record Group 59, National Archives, Washington, D.C., (hereinafter, L. D.).

11. *Id*. to *id*., Nov. 1, 1861, L. D., Vol. LXXVIII.

12. Dudley to Seward, Jan. 24, 1862, C. D., Liverpool, Vol. XX.

13. *Id.* to *id.,* Feb. 14, 1862, C. D., Liverpool, Vol. XX.

14. *Id.* to *id.,* Feb. 17, 1862, C. D., Liverpool, Vol. XX.

15. Adams to John Russell, Feb. 18, 1862, Notes to the British Government, State Department, Record Group 59, National Archives, Washington, D.C., (hereinafter, Notes to Britain).

16. Dudley to Seward, Feb. 19, 1862, C. D., Liverpool, Vol. XX.

17. Miller to Edwards, Feb. 21, 1862, Vol. MCCCXIII, FO5.

18. C. Morgan to Collector of Customs, Feb. 21, 1862, and Thomas F. Freemantle and Grenville C. L. Berkley to the Lords Commissioners of Her Majesty's Treasury, Feb. 22, 1862, Vol. MCCCXIII, FO5.

19. Russell to Adams, Feb. 26, 1862, L. D., Vol. LXXIX.

20. Dudley to Seward, Mar. 5 and Mar. 22, 1862, C. D. Liverpool, Vol. XX.

21. James Hudson to Russell, Mar. 25, 1862, Vol. MCCCXIII, FO5.

22. Russell to Adams, Mar. 26, 1862, Vol. MCCCXIII, FO5.

23. Statement of Thomas Robertson on board the *Oreto,* dated Apr., 1863, Civil War Claims.

24. Statement of Thomas Gill on board the *Oreto,* dated Apr. 20, 1863, Civil War Claims.

25. Samuel Whiting to Seward, Apr. 20, 1862, C. D., Nassau N. P., Vol. XI.

26. Whiting to C. J. Bayley, May 12, 1862, C. D., Nassau N. P., Vol. XI.

27. C. R. Nesbitt to Whiting, May 12, 1862, C. D. Nassau N. P., Vol. XI.

28. H. F. McKillop to Sir Alexander Milne, Apr. 20, 1862, Vol. MCCCXIII, FO5.

29. Bayley to McKillop, June 2, 1862, Vol. MCCCXIII, FO5.

30. Extract from the minutes of Executive Council of the Bahamas, June 4, 1862, Vol. MCCCXIII, FO5.

31. File on the *Oreto* in Bahamas, Attorney General's opinion in reference to the report of Captain McKillop of June 6, 1862, Vol. MCCCXIII, FO5.

32. H. D. Hinckley to Bayley, June 12, 1862, Vol. MCCCXIII, FO5.

33. Statement of Thomas Robertson, Apr., 1863, Civil War Claims.

34. Hinckley to Bayley, June 15, 1862, Vol. MCCCXIII, FO5.

35. Bayley to Hinckley, June 16, 1862, Vol. MCCCXIII, FO5.

36. G. L. Anderson's report on Hinckley's seizure of the *Oreto,* June 16, 1862, Vol. MCCCXIII, FO5.

37. Bayley to Hinckley, June 17, 1862, Vol. MCCCXIII, FO5.

38. Whiting to Hinckley, June 24, 1862, Vol. MCCCXIII, FO5.

39. Hinckley to Whiting, June 25, 1862, Vol. MCCCXIII, FO5.

40. Bayley to the Duke of Newcastle, June 26, 1862, Vol. MCCCXIII, FO5.

41. Dudley to Collector of Customs Liverpool, July 9, 1863, L. D., Vol. LXXXII.

42. Adams to Russell, Oct. 9, 1862, Notes to Britain.

43. Guert Gansevoort to Gideon Welles, Aug. 4, 1862, Letters from Admirals, Commodores and Captains, Vol. July–August 1862, III, Navy Records, Record Group 45, National Archives, Washington, D.C., (hereinafter, Letters of A. C. C.).

44. Whiting to Seward, July 31, 1862, C. D., Nassau N. P., Vol. XI.

45. *Id.* to *id.,* Aug. 1, 1862, C. D., Nassau N. P., Vol. XI.

46. John C. Lees, *Decree of His Honor John Campbell Lees, Esquire, Judge of the Vice-Admiralty Court of the Bahamas, in the case of the British Steamship Oreto, seized for the alleged violation of the Foreign Enlistment Act. Delivered 2nd Day of August, AD 1862, Nassau N. P. Bahamas* (Nassau, 1862), Enclosure in Whiting to Seward, Aug. 18, 1862, C. D., Nassau N. P., Vol. XII.

47. Whiting to Seward, Aug. 18, 1862, C. D., Nassau N. P., Vol. XII.

48. J. N. Maffitt's Journal, *ORN,* Series I, II, 669.

49. Frank L. Owsley, *King Cotton Diplomacy Foreign Relations of the Confederate States of America* (Chicago, 1959), 2nd ed., p. 407.

50. Whiting to Seward, July 31, 1862, C. D., Nassau N. P., Vol. XI.

51. Gansevoort to Welles, Aug. 4, 1862, Letters of A. C. C., Vol. July–August 1862, III.

52. Bulloch, *Secret Service,* I, 163–4.

53. Maffitt's Journal, pp. 8–9, Maffitt Papers, Southern Historical Collections, University of North Carolina.

54. Bulloch, *Secret Service,* I, 164–6.

55. Whiting to Seward, Aug. 9, 1862, C. D., Nassau N. P., Vol. XII ; and Maffitt's Journal, p. 9, Maffitt Papers.

56. Maffitt's Journal, *ORN,* Series I, I, 764.

57. Log of the *Florida,* Aug. 17–18, 1862, Navy Records, Record Group 45, National Archives, Washington, D.C., (hereinafter, Log of the *Florida,* Navy Records). In keeping the Log of the *Florida,* a "rough" copy was made and later recorded into a ledger as a so-called "smooth" copy. Part of both copies have been lost and the remaining parts divided between two different collections in

the National Archives, Navy Records (Record Group 45) and Records Relating to Civil War Claims (Record Group 76). In addition to these parts, Midshipman George D. Bryan made a copy of a part of the *Florida's* Log and the Log of the *Lapwing*. By combining all of these parts it was possible to reconstruct almost the entire Log of the *Florida*.

CHAPTER TWO

1. Maffitt's Journal, *ORN,* Series I, II, 667–8 ; and *ORN,* Series II, I, 247, 252.

2. Napoleon Collins to Welles, Nov. 17, 1864, Letters from Commanders, Vol. October–December 1864 IV, Navy Records, Record Group 45, National Archives, Washington, D.C., (hereinafter, Commanders Letters) ; statement of William E. Geoghegan, Smithsonian Institution, Washington, D.C.

3. Emma M. Maffitt, *The Life and Services of John Newland Maffitt* (New York, 1905), *passim,* (hereinafter, Maffitt, *Life of Maffitt*) ; and Maffitt's Journal, *passim,* Maffitt Papers.

4. Maffitt to Bulloch, Aug. 20, 1862, *ORN,* Series I, I, 760 ; and Log of the *Florida,* Aug. 17, 1862, Navy Records.

5. Maffitt's Journal, Aug. 18–30, 1862, *ORN,* Series I, I, 765.

6. Log of the *Florida,* Aug. 17–31, 1862, Navy Records ; and Maffitt's Journal, Aug. 22–30, 1862, *ORN,* Series I, I, 765.

7. Maffitt's Journal, Sept. 1, 1862, *ORN,* Series I, I, 766.

8. Log of the *Florida,* Sept. 2–3, 1862, Navy Records.

9. *Ibid.,* Sept. 4, 1862, Navy Records ; and Maffitt, *Life of Maffitt,* pp. 253–4.

10. George Preble to D. G. Farragut, Sept. 10, 1862, *ORN,* Series I, I, 436–40.

11. Log of the *Florida,* Sept. 4, 1862, Navy Records.

12. Preble to Farragut, Sept. 4, 1862, *ORN,* Series I, I, 432.

13. "Abstract of Log of *U.S.S. Oneida,* Commander George H. Preble, Sept. 4, 1862," *ORN,* Series I, I, 432–3.

14. H. W. Wilson, "Cruise of the Oneida—a diary," Sept. 4, 1862, Southern Historical Collection, University of North Carolina.

15. Welles to President Lincoln, Feb. 10, 1863, Executive Letter Book, the Secretary of the Navy, XVI, Navy Records, Record Group 45, National Archives, Washington, D.C., (hereinafter, Executive Letter Book).

16. Maffitt, *Life of Maffitt,* pp. 383, 411.

17. Maffitt's Journal, *ORN,* Series I, I, 767.

18. Log of the *Florida,* Sept. 7–12, 1862, Navy Records.
19. *Ibid.,* Sept. 8–30, 1862, Navy Records.
20. Maffitt's Journal, *ORN,* Series I, I, 767.
21. Log of the *Florida,* Oct. 1, 1862–Jan. 6, 1863, Navy Records.
22. Maffitt's Journal, pp. 23–5, Maffitt Papers.
23. Maffitt's Journal, Dec. 1, 1863, *ORN,* Series I, I, 768–9.
24. Maffitt's Journal, p. 27, Maffitt Papers.
25. Franklin Buchanan to Mallory, Jan. 1, 1863, Buchanan-Screven Papers, Southern Historical Collection, University of North Carolina.
26. Maffitt's Journal, p. 27, Maffitt Papers.
27. *Times* (London), Feb. 17, 1863 ; and Maffitt, *Life of Maffitt,* pp. 136–7.
28. *Ibid.,* pp. 136–96 ; and Joseph T. Durkin, *Stephen R. Mallory: Confederate Navy Chief* (Chapel Hill, 1954), pp. 70–83.
29. Log of the *Florida,* Sept. 30, 1862–Jan. 11, 1863, Navy Records ; and Maffitt's Journal, pp. 27–8, Maffitt Papers.
30. Payroll of Allotments granted on board the *CSS Florida* payable at the Naval Station at New Orleans, Oct. 10, 1862 ; and Allotment Records of the *Florida,* November, 1862, to January, 1863, Navy Records, Record Group 45, National Archives, Washington, D.C.
31. Maffitt's Journal, p. 24, Maffitt Papers.
32. Mallory to Maffitt, Oct. 25, 1862, Maffitt, *Life of Maffitt,* pp. 263–4.
33. Buchanan to Maffitt, Jan. 6, 1863, Buchanan-Screven Papers.
34. Log of the *Florida,* Jan. 11–13, 1863, Navy Records.
35. Maffitt's Journal, *ORN,* Series I, II, 667.
36. Maffitt's Journal, pp. 28–9; Maffitt Papers.
37. Maffitt's Journal, *ORN,* Series I, II, 667–8.
38. George F. Emmons to Welles, Feb. 10, 1863, Vol. January–February 1863 I, Commanders Letters.
39. Emmons to R. B. Hitchcock, Mar. 12, 1863, *ORN,* Series I, II, 30–1.
40. Portions of this chapter have appeared in Frank L. Owsley, Jr., "The C.S.S. *Florida's* Tour de Force at Mobile Bay," *The Alabama Review,* XV, pp. 262–270 (October, 1962).

CHAPTER THREE

1. Log of the *Florida,* Jan. 16, 1863, Navy Records.
2. *Ibid.,* Jan. 19, 1863, Navy Records.

3. Statement of John Brown, Captain of the *Estelle,* Jan. 21, 1863, C. D. Havana, Vol. XLVI.

4. Maffitt's Journal, pp. 29–31, Maffitt Papers ; and Maffitt, *Life of Maffitt,* p. 274.

5. R. W. Shufeldt to Seward, Jan. 21 and 22, 1863, C. D. Havana, Vol. XLVI.

6. Maffitt's Journal, p. 30, Maffitt Papers.

7. Protest of the Master of the *Windward,* Richard Roberts, C. D. Havana, Vol. XLVI.

8. Statement of Frederick H. Small, Master of the ship *Corris Ann,* C. D. Havana, Vol. XLVI.

9. Maffitt's Journal, *ORN,* Series I, II, 668.

10. Log of the *Florida,* Jan. 23–26, 1863, Navy Records.

11. Maffitt's Journal, *ORN,* Series I, II, 660 ; Bayley to Maffitt, Jan. 26, 1863, enclosure in Seward to Adams, Mar. 28, 1863, Post Records London, State Department, Records of Foreign Posts, Record Group 84, National Archives, Washington, D.C. (hereinafter, Post Records).

12. Maffitt's Journal, pp. 31–2, Maffitt Papers.

13. Maffitt's Journal, *ORN,* Series I, II, 669.

14. Log of the *Florida,* Jan. 26–27, 1863, Navy Records.

15. Maffitt's Journal, *ORN,* Series I, II, 669.

16. *Times* (London), Mar. 6, 1863.

17. Maffitt's Journal, p. 33, Maffitt Papers.

18. Log of the *Florida,* Feb. 9–11, 1863, Navy Records.

19. Maffitt, *Life of Maffitt,* p. 275.

20. Log of the *Florida,* Feb. 12, 1863, Navy Records.

21. Maffitt, *Life of Maffitt,* pp. 274–5 ; and Maffitt's Journal, pp. 33–5, Maffitt Papers ; and Maffitt to Preble, Apr. 11, 1880, Edward Boykin, *Sea Devil of the Confederacy* (New York, 1959), pp. 295–6.

22. Log of the *Florida,* Feb. 12–24, 1863, Navy Records.

23. Maffitt's Journal, pp. 35–6, Maffitt Papers.

24. Maffitt's Journal, *ORN,* Series I, II, 670.

25. Maffitt's Journal, pp. 36–7, Maffitt Papers.

26. Maffitt's Journal, *ORN,* Series I, II, 670.

27. Edward Throwbridge to Seward, Feb. 25, 1863, C. D. Barbados, Vol. X.

28. Throwbridge to John T. Edgar, Feb. 24, 1863, C. D. Barbados, Vol. X.

29. Seward to Adams, Mar. 23, 1863, Post Records.

30. Log of the *Florida,* Feb. 25–26, 1863, Navy Records.

31. Report of C. W. Quinn to Maffitt, Feb. 14, 1863, Maffitt Papers.

32. Log of the *Florida,* Feb. 27–Mar. 6, 1863, Navy Records.

33. Maffitt, *Life of Maffitt,* pp. 279–80.

34. Log of the *Florida,* Mar. 7–12, 1863, Navy Records.

35. Maffitt, *Life of Maffitt,* pp. 279–80.

36. *Royal Gazette* (Hamilton, Bermuda), Mar. 31, 1863.

37. Maffitt, *Life of Maffitt,* p. 280.

38. Seward to Adams, Mar. 9, 1863, Instructions to Great Britain, Vol. XVIII.

39. *New York Times,* Jan. 30, 1863.

40. Charles Wilkes to Welles, Jan. 23, 1863, Letters from Officers Commanding Squadrons: West India Squadron, Vol. I, Navy Records, Record Group 45, National Archives, Washington, D.C., (hereinafter, Letters of W. I. Squadron).

41. C. H. Baldwin to Welles, Feb. 20, 1863, Letters of W. I. Squadron, Vol. I.

42. Welles to J. F. DuPont, Jan. 21, 1863, Confidential Letters Sent, Vol. V, Navy Records, Record Group 45, National Archives, Washington, D.C.

43. Welles to Seward, Mar. 17, 1863, Executive Letter Book, Vol. XVI.

44. Log of the *Florida,* Mar. 6–27, 1863, and *passim,* Navy Records; and Maffitt's Journal, Maffitt Papers, *passim.*

45. Log of the *Florida,* Mar. 28, 1863, Navy Records; and Maffitt, *Life of Maffitt,* p. 281.

46. George D. Bryan, Abstract of the Log of the *Florida* and Log of the *Lapwing,* Mar. 30–Apr. 15, 1863, Navy Records, Record Group 45, National Archives, Washington, D.C., (hereinafter, Log of the *Florida* and *Lapwing,* Navy Records).

47. Maffitt's Journal, *ORN,* Series I, II, 671–3.

48. Statement of George T. Brown, enclosure in O. S. Glisson to Welles, May 21, 1863, Letters of A. C. C., Vol. May 1863, IV.

49. Maffitt's Journal, *ORN,* Series I, II, 673.

50. Statement of James T. Potter, enclosure in Glisson to Welles, May 21, 1863, Letters of A. C. C., Vol. May 1863, IV.

51. Maffitt, *Life of Maffitt,* p. 287.

52. Antonio Gomez Leal to Maffitt, May 1, 1863, *ORN,* Series I, II, 643–4.

53. Log of the *Florida,* May 2–4, 1863, Navy Records.

54. Maffitt, *Life of Maffitt,* p. 287.

55. Maffitt to Bulloch, Apr. 25, 1863 (captured letter), L. D. Britain, Vol. LXXXIII.

56. *New York Times,* Mar. 29, 1863.

57. Henry Forster & Co. to Welles, Apr. 20, 1863, Miscellaneous Letters Received, Vol. April 1863, III, Navy Records, Record Group 45, National Archives, Washington, D.C., (hereinafter, Miscellaneous Letters).

58. Glisson to Welles, May 20, 1863, Letters of A. C. C., Vol. May 1863, IV.

59. *Id.* to *id.,* May 21, 1863, Letters of A. C. C., Vol. May 1863, IV.

60. Wilkes to Welles, Apr. 16, 1863, Letters of W. I. Squadron, Vol. I.

61. Log of the *Florida,* May 7–8, 1863, Navy Records.

62. Maffitt, *Life of Maffitt,* pp. 292–4.

63. Glisson to Welles, May 20, 1863, Letters of A. C. C., Vol. May 1863, IV.

64. Log of the *Florida,* May 8–12, 1863, Navy Records.

65. Joao Silverra de Sousa to Thomas W. Adamson, Jr., May 9, 1863, C. D. Pernambuco, Brazil, Vol. VII.

66. H. H. Swift & Co. to Welles, June 24, 1863, Miscellaneous Letters, Vol. June 1863, III.

67. Webb to Marquis D'Abrantes, May 27, 1863, L. D. Brazil, Vol. XXVIII.

68. Adamson to Seward, June 10, 1863, C. D. Pernambuco, Brazil, Vol. VII ; and Maffitt, *Life of Maffitt,* p. 295.

69. Maffitt to Mallory, July 27, 1863, *ORN,* Series I, II, 652.

70. Log of the *Florida* and *Lapwing,* Mar. 30–Apr. 15, 1863, Navy Records.

71. Maffitt, *Life of Maffitt,* pp. 281–7.

72. G. Terry Sinclair, "The Eventful Cruise of the *Florida,*" *The Century Magazine,* LVI, pp. 421–3 (July, 1898), (hereinafter, Sinclair, "Cruise of the *Florida*").

73. Log of the *Florida* and *Lapwing,* Apr. 17–20, 1863, Navy Records.

74. Edward A. Sander & Co. to Welles, June 13, 1863, Miscellaneous Letters, Vol. June 1863 II.

75. Log of the *Florida* and *Lapwing,* Apr. 21–May 5, 1863, Navy Records.

76. Maffitt, *Life of Maffitt,* p. 281.

77. C. H. Baldwin to Welles, July 23, 1863, *ORN,* Series I, II, 407–8.

78. Sinclair, "Cruise of the *Florida,*" pp. 421–3.

79. Log of the *Florida,* May 15–31, 1863, Navy Records.

80. Maffitt to Mallory, July 27, 1863, *ORN,* Series I, II, 652–3.

81. Log of the *Florida,* May 20, 1863, Navy Records.
82. Maffitt, *Life of Maffitt,* p. 297.
83. Adamson to Seward, July 23, 1863, C. D. Pernambuco, Brazil, Vol. VII.
84. Maffitt to Mallory, July 27, 1863, *ORN,* Series I, II, 653.
85. Maffitt, *Life of Maffitt,* p. 298.
86. *Post* (Boston), Aug. 13, 1863.
87. Seward to Adams, Aug. 22, 1863, Instructions to Great Britain, Vol. XVIII.
88. Maffitt to Mallory, July 27, 1863, *ORN,* Series I, II, 653.
89. Maffitt, *Life of Maffitt,* pp. 298–9.
90. Maffitt to Mallory, July 27, 1863, *ORN,* Series I, II, 653.
91. W. C. J. Hyland to Seward, July 25, 1863, C. D. Bermuda, Vol. VI.
92. Dudley to Seward, Aug. 22, 1863, C. D. Liverpool, Vol. XXV.
93. Mallory to Maffitt, Aug. 27, 1863, *ORN,* Series I, II, 657-9.
94. Maffitt, *Life of Maffitt,* pp. 299–300.
95. *Times* (London), July 27, 1863.
96. Maffitt to Mallory, June 27, 1863, *ORN,* Series I, II, 653.
97. Maffitt, *Life of Maffitt,* pp. 298–9.
98. Maffitt to Mallory, July 27, 1863, *ORN,* Series I, II, 653.
99. Maffitt, *Life of Maffitt,* pp. 298–9.
100. J. N. Miller to Welles, July 9, 1863, *ORN,* Series I, II, 383–4.
101. Miller to Welles, July 13, 1863, *ORN,* Series I, II, 384–5.
102. Maffitt to Mallory, July 27, 1863, *ORN,* Series I, II, 653–4.
103. Welles to John B. Montgomery, July 10, 1863, *ORN,* Series I, II, 385.
104. Maffitt, *Life of Maffitt,* p. 303.
105. Maffitt to Mallory, July 27, 1863, *ORN,* Series I, II, 653–4.
106. George Ord to the Duke of Newcastle, Aug. 3, 1863, FO5, Vol. MCCCXIV.
107. William Munro to Major Nugent, Aug. 7, 1863, FO5, Vol. MCCCXIV.
108. Maffitt to Mallory, July 27, 1863, *ORN,* Series I, II, 653–4.
109. Hyland to Seward, July 27, 1863, C. D. Bermuda, Vol. XXVII.
110. Maffitt, *Life of Maffitt,* p. 309.
111. Maffitt to Mallory, Sept. (no day given), 1863, *ORN,* Series I, II, 659.
112. Maffitt to John Slidell, Aug. 18, 1863, *ORN,* Series I, II, 658–9.

113. *Times* (London), Aug. 21, 1863.
114. Statement of Evan Evans, Aug. 25, 1863, FO5, Vol. MCCCXIV.
115. *Times* (London), Aug. 31, 1863.

CHAPTER FOUR

1. Read to Maffitt, May 6, 1863, *ORN,* Series I, II, 644.
2. Maffitt to Read, May 6, 1863, *ORN,* Series I, II, 645.
3. Read to Mallory, Oct. 19, 1864, *ORN,* Series I, II, 655.
4. *New York Times,* June 29, 1863.
5. Read to Mallory, Oct. 19, 1864, *ORN,* Series I, II, 655.
6. *Id.* to *id.,* Oct. 19, 1864, *ORN,* Series I, II, 655–6.
7. Edward A. Sander & Co. to Welles, June 13, 1863, Miscellaneous Letters, Vol. June 1863, II.
8. Read to Mallory, Oct. 19, 1864, *ORN,* Series I, II, 656.
9. Edward A. Sander & Co. to Welles, June 13, 1863, Miscellaneous Letters, Vol. June 1863, II.
10. Read to Mallory, Oct. 19, 1864, *ORN,* Series I, II, 656.
11. Edward A. Sander & Co. to Welles, June 13, 1863, Miscellaneous Letters, Vol. June 1863, II.
12. Read to Mallory, Oct. 19, 1864, *ORN,* Series I, II, 656.
13. N. E. Smith and Sons to Welles, June 22, 1863, Miscellaneous Letters, Vol. June 1863, III.
14. Read to Mallory, Oct. 19, 1864, *ORN,* Series I, II, 656.
15. Sturges, Clearman & Co., New York, to Welles, June 27, 1864, Miscellaneous Letters, Vol. June 1863, III.
16. Read to Mallory, Oct. 19, 1864, *ORN,* Series I, II, 656.
17. *New York Times,* June 29, 1863.
18. Read to Mallory, Oct. 19, 1864, *ORN,* Series I, II, 656.
19. Extract of Read's notebook, enclosure in letter from George L. Andrews to Edwin M. Stanton, June 27, 1863, Miscellaneous Letters, Vol. June, 1863, III.
20. Read to Mallory, Oct. 19, 1864, *ORN,* Series I, II, 656.
21. Extract of Read's notebook, enclosure in letter from Andrews to Stanton, June 27, 1963. Miscellaneous Letters, Vol. June 1863, III.
22. Welles to Alpheus, Hardy & Co., July 3, 1863, Miscellaneous Letters Sent (General Letter Book), Vol. LXXI, Navy Records, Record Group 45, National Archives, Washington, D.C., (hereinafter, Miscellaneous Letters Sent).
23. *New York Times,* June 28, 1863 ; and Read to Mallory, Oct. 19, 1864, *ORN,* Series I, II, 656.

24. Petition from Boston merchants to Navy Department, June 25, 1863, Miscellaneous Letters, Vol. June 1863, III.

25. Samuel Ober and fourteen others to Welles, June 24, 1863, Miscellaneous Letters, Vol. June 1863, III.

26. John Andrew to Welles, July 16, 1863, *ORN,* Series I, II, 347–8 ; and Welles to Andrew, July 18, 1863, Miscellaneous Letters Sent, Vol. LXXI.

27. Welles to Andrew, July 11, 1863, and Welles to M. Mack, July 1, 1863, Miscellaneous Letters Sent, Vol. LXXI.

28. E. D. Morgan to Welles, June 23, 1863, Miscellaneous Letters, Vol. June 1863, III.

29. S. M. Felton to Welles, June 16, 1863, Miscellaneous Letters, Vol. June 1863, II.

30. Felton to Welles, June 26, 1863, Miscellaneous Letters, Vol. June 1863, III.

31. Welles to Andrew, July 11, 1863, Miscellaneous Letters Sent, Vol. LXXI.

32. *Id.* to *id.,* Aug. 17, 1863, Miscellaneous Letters Sent, Vol. LXXII.

33. S. P. Lee to Welles, June 18 and June 20, 1863, Letters from Officers Commanding Squadrons: North Atlantic Blockading Squadron, Vol. III, Navy Records, Record Group 45, National Archives, Washington, D.C., (hereinafter, Letters of N. A. B. S.).

34. *Ibid ;* and Henry Rolando to Welles, June 21, 1863, Commanders Letters, Vol. May–June 1863, III.

35. M. Jackson to Navy Department, June 27, 1863, Miscellaneous Letters, Vol. June 1863, III.

36. Welles to the Master of the *Le Roy* of Baltimore, June 24, 1863, Miscellaneous Letters Sent, Vol. LXXI.

37. Thomas H. Patterson to Welles, July 1, 1863, Commanders Letters, Vol. July–August 1863, IV.

38. Read to Mallory, Oct. 19, 1864, *ORN,* Series I, II, 656–7.

39. Jedediah Jewett to Salmon P. Chase, June 27, 1863, *ORN,* Series I, II, 322–3 ; and Jewett to Chase, Letterbook of Jedediah Jewett, Collector of Customs, Portland, Maine, Treasury Records, Record Group 56, National Archives, Washington, D.C., (hereinafter, Jewett Letterbook).

40. Read to Mallory, Oct. 19, 1864, *ORN,* Series I, II, 656–7.

41. Jewett to Chase, June 27, 1863, *ORN,* Series I, II, 323.

42. Read to Mallory, Oct. 19, 1864, *ORN,* Series I, II, 656–7.

43. Jewett to Chase, June 27, 1863, *ORN,* Series I, II, 323.

44. Read to Mallory, Oct. 19, 1864, *ORN,* Series I, II, 656–7.

45. Jewett to Chase, June 27, 1863, *ORN,* Series I, II, 323.

46.   Read to Mallory, Oct. 19, 1864, *ORN*, Series I, II, 657.
47.   Jewett to Chase, June 27, 1863, *ORN*, Series I, II, 324–5.
48.   J. H. Merryman to Chase, June 29, 1863, *ORN*, Series I, II, 365–6.
49.   Jewett to Chase, June 27 and July 1, 1863, *ORN*, Series I, II, 324–5 and 329.
50.   Read to Mallory, July 30, 1863, *ORN*, Series I, II, 654–5.
51.   Jewett to Chase, June 27, 1863, *ORN*, Series I, II, 324.
52.   Jim Dan Hill, *Sea Dogs of the Sixties* (Minneapolis, 1935), pp. 179–84.

CHAPTER FIVE

1.   Report of Harry Maircals to Earl Granville Concerning activities on the *Florida* 1863–64, Sept. 22, 1871, FO5, Vol. MCCCXIV, (hereinafter, Report of Harry Maircals, FO5).
2.   *Ibid.;* and *Norwich Weekly Courier* (Norwich, Conn.), Sept. 24, 1863.
3.   William L. Dayton to Seward, Sept. 17, 1863, L. D. France, Vol. LIII.
4.   Report of Harry Maircals, FO5, Vol. MCCCXIV.
5.   Dayton to Seward, Aug. 25, 1863, L. D. France, Vol. LIII.
6.   *Id.* to *id.*, Sept. 3, 1863, L. D. France, Vol. LIII.
7.   John Bigelow to Henry S. Sanford, Sept. 1, 1863, Sanford Papers, Sanford Memorial Library, Sanford, Florida.
8.   Joshua Nunn to Seward, Sept. 11, 1863, C. D. London, Vol. XXXII.
9.   Dayton to Seward, Sept. 17, 1863, L. D. France, Vol. LIII.
10.   Bigelow to Seward, Sept. 11, 1863, C. D. Paris, Vol. XIII.
11.   W. Grey to Russell, Sept. 11, 1863, FO5, Vol. MCCCXIV.
12.   Dayton to Seward, Sept. 17, 1863, L. D. France, Vol. LIII.
13.   *Id.* to *id.*, Oct. 27, 1863, L. D. France, Vol. LIV.
14.   Seward to Dayton, Oct. 24, 1863, Instructions to France, Vol. XVI.
15.   Grey to Russell, Sept. 11, 1863, FO5, Vol. MCCCXIV.
16.   Seward to Dayton, Nov. 21, 1863, Post Records Paris.
17.   *Id.* to *id.*, Nov. 10, 1863, Post Records Paris.
18.   Report of Harry Maircals, FO5, Vol. MCCCXIV.
19.   *New York Times*, Sept. 18, 1863.
20.   Log of the *Florida* and Morris to Samuel Barron, Feb. 1 and Feb. 9, 1864, Records relating to Civil War Claims United States and Great Britain, State Department, Record Group 76, National

Archives, Washington, D.C., (hereinafter, Log of the *Florida,* Civil War Claims).

21. Barney to Morris, Feb. 5, 1864, letters captured on the *Florida,* enclosure in Seward to Adams, Dec. 12, 1864, Post Records London.

22. Morris to Barron, Feb. 18, 1864, Civil War Claims.

23. Log of the *Florida,* Jan. 21–28, 1864, Civil War Claims.

24. Report of Harry Maircals, FO5, Vol. MCCCXIV.

25. A. Norus and Co. to Morris, Jan. 15 and Jan. 18, 1864, Letters captured on the *Florida,* enclosure in Seward to Adams, Dec. 21, 1864, Post Records London.

26. Morris to Barron, Feb. 19, 1864, Civil War Claims.

27. F. H. Morse to Consul Robinson, Jan. 21, 1864, C. D. London, Vol. XXXIII.

28. Log of the *Florida, passim,* Civil War Claims and Navy Records.

29. Maffitt to his family, Sept. 1, 1863, Maffitt Papers.

30. List of the crew of the *Florida,* which were paid off at Brest and Liverpool, Civil War Claims.

31. Log of the *Florida,* Oct. 1, 1863–Jan. 10, 1864, Civil War Claims.

32. Sinclair, "Cruise of the *Florida;*" and petition signed by fourteen members of the crew of the *Florida* to Maffitt, Sept. 16, 1863, Maffitt Papers; and Log of the *Florida,* Oct. 1, 1863–Jan. 1, 1864, Civil War Claims.

33. James Dyke to Maffitt, Nov. 15, 1864, Maffitt Papers.

34. *Times* (London), Sept. 18, 1863; and Maffitt's Journal, *passim,* Maffitt Papers.

35. Maffitt to Bulloch, Sept. 3, 1863, L. D. Britain, Vol. LXXXIV.

36. Dudley to Seward, Sept. 18, 1863, C. D. Liverpool, Vol. XXV.

37. *Daily Post* (Liverpool), Sept. 17, 1863.

38. Statement of William Thompson, Sept. (no day given), 1863, Civil War Claims.

39. Adams to Russell, Sept. 24, 1863, L. D. Britain, Vol. LXXXIV.

40. Maffitt to Bulloch, Sept. 3, 1863, C. D. Liverpool, Vol. XXV.

41. Welles to Seward, Oct. 16, 1863, Executive Letterbook, Vol. XVII.

42. Dayton to Seward, Mar. 4, 1864, L. D. France, Vol. LIV.

43. Dudley to Seward, Jan. 5, 1864, C. D. Liverpool, Vol. XXVI.

44. Bulloch to C. M. Morris, Jan. 14, 1864, Letters captured on the *Florida,* enclosure in Seward to Adams, Dec. 21, 1864, Post Records London.

45. Dayton to Seward, Oct. 8, 1863, L. D. France, Vol. LIII.
46. *Id.* to *id.*, Mar. 4, 1864, L. D. France, Vol. LII.
47. Log of the *Florida* and T. J. Charlton to J. N. Barney, Dec. 28, 1863, Civil War Claims ; and Sick Log of the *Florida,* Records relating to Civil War Claims United States and Great Britain, State Department, Record Group 76, National Archives, Washington, D.C.
48. Barron to Morris, Jan. 5, 1864, *ORN,* Series I, II, 662.
49. J. Thomas Scharf, *History of the Confederate States Navy from its Organization to the Surrender of its Last Vessel* (Albany, 1894), p. 792 ; and *Register of Officers of the Confederate States Navy 1861–1865* (Washington, 1931), p. 138.
50. Morris to Barron, Jan. 31, 1863, Civil War Claims.
51. *Id.* to *id.*, Feb. 9, 1864, Civil War Claims.
52. Barney to Morris, Feb. 5, 1864, letters captured on the *Florida,* enclosure in Seward to Adams, Dec. 21, 1864, Post Records London.
53. Log of the *Kearsarge,* Sept. 17, 1863, Navy Records, Record Group 45, National Archives, Washington, D.C., (hereinafter, Log of the *Kearsarge,* Navy Records).
54. J. A. Winslow to Welles, Sept. 18, 1863, Letters of A. C. C., Vol. September 1863, VIII.
55. Log of the *Kearsarge,* Sept. 17–23, 1864, Navy Records.
56. *Ibid.,* Sept. 24, 1863, Navy Records ; and Log of the *Florida,* Sept. 23, 1863, Civil War Claims.
57. Log of the *Florida,* Sept. 25–Oct. 8, 1863, Civil War Claims.
58. Log of the *Kearsarge,* Sept. 26–28, 1863, Navy Records.
59. Winslow to Dayton, Sept. 28, 1863, L. D. France, Vol. LIII.
60. Winslow to Welles, Oct. 9, 1863, Letters of A. C. C., Vol. October 1863, IX.
61. Log of the *Florida,* Oct. 9, 1863, Civil War Claims.
62. Edwin G. Eastman to Sanford, Nov. 7, 1863, and Jan. 21, 1864, Sanford Papers.
63. Welles to Seward, Sept. 21, 1863, Executive Letter Book, Vol. XVI.
64. Dayton to Winslow, Oct. 21, 1863, L. D. Paris, Vol. LIII.
65. Winslow to Welles, Oct. 21, 1863, Letters of A. C. C., Vol. October 1863, IX.
66. Log of the *Kearsarge,* Nov. 1–8, 1863, Navy Records ; and Winslow to Welles, Nov. 7, 1863, Letters of A. C. C., Vol. November 1863, X.
67. Log of the *Kearsarge,* Nov. 7–Dec. 5, 1863, Navy Records.
68. Report of Harry Maircals, FO5, Vol. MCCCXIV.
69. Log of the *Kearsarge,* Nov. 7–Dec. 5, 1863, Navy Records.

70. Dayton to Winslow, Nov. 30, 1863, *ORN*, Series I, II, 510–11.
71. Log of the *Kearsarge*, Dec. 5–10, 1863, Navy Records.
72. Winslow to Welles, Dec. 11, 1863, Letters of A. C. C., Vol. December 1863, XI; and Log of the *Florida*, Dec. 26-29, 1863, Civil War Claims; and Log of the *Kearsarge*, Dec. 29, 1863–Feb. 14, 1864, Navy Records.
73. Log of the *Florida*, Feb. 10, 1864, Navy Records.
74. F. H. Morse to Seward, Jan. 23, 1864, C. D. London, Vol. XXXIII.

CHAPTER SIX

1. Log of the *Florida*, Feb. 10, 1864, Navy Records.
2. Morris to Barron, Feb. 18, 1864, Civil War Claims.
3. Log of the *Florida*, Feb. 16, 1864, Navy Records.
4. Morris to Barron, Feb. 18, 1864, Civil War Claims.
5. Log of the *Florida*, Feb. 19, 1864, Navy Records.
6. Winslow to Welles, Feb. 19, 1864, Letters of A. C. C., Vol. January–February 1864, I.
7. *Id.* to *id.*, Mar. 21, 1864, Letters of A. C. C., Vol. March–April 1864, II.
8. Preble to Welles, Feb. 14, 1864, Commanders Letters, Vol. January–March 1864, I.
9. *Id.* to *id.*, Feb. 28, 1864, Commanders Letters, Vol. January–March 1864, I.
10. *Id.* to *id.*, Mar. 1, 1864, Commanders Letters, Vol. January–March 1864, I.
11. *Id.* to *id.*, May 2, 1864, Commanders Letters, Vol. April–June 1864, II.
12. *Id.* to *id.*, Mar. 1, 1864, Commanders Letters, Vol. January–March 1864, I.
13. Log of the *Florida*, Feb. 20–27, 1864, Civil War Claims.
14. Morris to Joaquin Pedro de Castelbrance, Feb. 28, 1864, Civil War Claims.
15. Castelbrance to Morris, Feb. 28, 1864, Civil War Claims.
16. Morris to Castelbrance, Feb. 29, 1864, Civil War Claims.
17. Morris to Barron, Feb. 29, 1864, Civil War Claims.
18. Robert Baymen to James E. Harvey, March 18, 1864, and Harvey to Seward, May 4, 1864, *Papers Relating to Foreign Affairs* (38th Congress, Second Session, House Document, Serial 1219) (Washington, 1865), IV, 298, 308–9.
19. Log of the *Florida*, Feb. 29–Mar. 5, 1864, Navy Records.

20. Preble to Welles, Mar. 7, 1864, Commanders Letters, Vol. January–March 1864, I.

21. Log of the *Florida,* Mar. 6–28, 1864, Navy Records.

22. *Ibid.,* Apr. 4–26, 1864, Navy Records.

23. Morse to Seward, Mar. 4, 1864, C. D. London, XXXIII.

24. *Times* (London), Apr. 15, 1864.

25. Log of the *Florida,* Apr. 26–30, 1864, Navy Records.

26. Charlton to Morris, Apr. 26, 1864, Sick Log of the *Florida,* Civil War Claims.

27. Morris to Mallory, Apr. 29, 1864, Civil War Claims.

28. Interview with W. S. Hoole, Librarian at the University of Alabama, a relative of James L. Hoole.

29. Morris to J. C. Lake, Apr. 28, 1864, Civil War Claims.

30. Morris to Mallory, May 11, 1864, Civil War Claims.

31. James L. Lardner to Welles, May 10, and June 11, 1864, Letters of W. I. Squadron, Vol. II.

32. Welles to C. R. P. Rogers, May 18, 1864, Confidential Letters Sent, Vol. V, Navy Records, Record Group 45, National Archives, Washington, D.C.

33. Log of the *Florida,* May 1–12, 1864, Navy Records.

34. Morris to Mallory, May 12, 1864, Civil War Claims.

35. Charlton to Morris, June 19, 1864, Sick Log of the *Florida,* Civil War Claims.

36. Morris to Mallory, May 12, 1864, Civil War Claims.

37. Quinn to Morris, May 10, 1864, Civil War Claims.

38. Log of the *Florida,* May 18–June 17, 1864, Navy Records.

39. Morris to Mallory, June 21, 1864, Civil War Claims.

40. Confidential Communication to be made to the officer in command of the *Florida* from Vice Admiral James Hope, June 19, 1864, Civil War Claims.

41. Morris to J. W. Ashby, June 21, 1864, Civil War Claims.

42. Morris to Hope, June 14, 1864, Civil War Claims.

43. Quinn to Morris, June 15, 1864, Civil War Claims.

44. Log of the *Florida,* June 20, 1864, Navy Records.

45. Morris to William Munroe, June 21, 1864, Civil War Claims.

46. Morris to Mallory, June 19, 1864, *ORN,* Series I, II, 615.

47. *Id.* to *id.,* June 27, 1864, Civil War Claims.

48. *Id.* to *id.,* June 28, 1864, Civil War Claims.

49. Mallory to Morris, June 2, 1864, *ORN,* Series I, III, 612–13.

50. Morris to Mallory, June 27, 1864, Civil War Claims.

51. Mallory to Morris, June 2, 1864, *ORN,* Series I, III, 612–13.

52. Log of the *Florida,* June 28–29, 1864, Navy Records.

53. Log of the *Florida,* July 1–2, 1864, Civil War Claims.

54. Morris to Mallory, July 3, 1864, Civil War Claims. It is not believed that the W. H. Jackson signed on by Morris was the same W. H. Jackson relieved from the *Florida* by Maffitt.

55. Adams to Russell, August 19, 1864, *Papers Relating to Foreign Affairs* (38th Congress, Second Session, House Document, Serial 1217), II, 293.

56. Seward to Adams, July 29, 1864, Instructions to Britain.

57. Russell to Adams, Aug. 22, 1864, *Papers Relating to Foreign Affairs* (38th Congress, Second Session, House Document, Serial 1217), II, 293.

58. Journal of Midshipman C. C. Cary, Records relating to Civil War Claims United States and Great Britain, State Department, Record Group 76, National Archives, Washington, D.C.

59. Log of the *Florida,* July 7–9, 1864, Navy Records.

60. Morris to Mallory, July 13, 1864, Civil War Claims.

61. Log of the *Florida,* July 10, 1864, Navy Records.

62. Morris to Mallory, July 13, 1864, Civil War Claims.

63. Log of the Florida, July 10, 1864, Navy Records.

64. Morris to Mallory, July 13, 1864, Civil War Claims.

65. William J. Taylor and Co. to Welles, July 15, 1864, Miscellaneous Letters, Vol. July 1864.

66. Morris to Mallory, July 13, 1864, Civil War Claims ; and Sinclair, "The Cruise of the *Florida,*" p. 424.

67. S. P. Lee to Welles, July 10, 1864, Letters of the N. A. B. S., Vol. III.

68. G. V. Fox to George W. Blunt, July 23, 1864, Miscellaneous Letters, Vol. July 1864.

69. S. W. Gordon to Welles, Aug. 24, 1864, Letters of A.C.C., Vol. July–August 1864, IV.

70. Morris to Mallory, July 13, 1864, Civil War Claims.

71. Charles Steedman to Welles, Aug. 5, 1864, and Dan B. Ridgley to Lee, July 25, 1864, Letters of A. C. C., Vol. July–August 1864, IV.

72. Sam Corey to Welles, July 18, 1864, Miscellaneous Letters, Vol. July 1864.

73. J. Taylor Wood to Mallory, Aug. 31, 1864, *ORN,* Series I, III, 701–4.

74. A. L. Drayton to Welles, June 12, 1864, Miscellaneous Letters, Vol. July 1864 ; and Jewett to Chase, June 30, 1863, Jewett Letterbook.

75. Welles to Stephen Cabot, July 19, 1864, Miscellaneous Letters Sent, Vol. LXXIV.

76. Welles to Steedman, July 23, 1864, Confidential Letters, Vol. V.

77. Welles to Cabot, July 22, 1864, Miscellaneous Letters Sent, Vol. LXXIV.

78. Welles to Drayton, July 23, 1864, Confidential Letters, Vol. V.

79. Log of the *Florida,* July 11–Aug. 4, 1864, Navy Records.

80. Morris to Mallory, Aug. 4, 1864, Civil War Claims.

81. Log of the *Florida,* Aug. 22–Sept. 10, 1864, Navy Records.

82. It is unknown whether or not Lieutenant T. K. Porter had any defense against these allegations. His personal papers are in the possession of his family in Montgomery, Alabama, but unfortunately this author was not permitted to examine them.

83. Copy of unsigned note, written into the Log of the *Florida,* Navy Records.

84. Morris to T. K. Porter, Sept. 19, 1864, Civil War Claims.

85. Log of the *Florida,* Sept. 23–Oct. 1, 1864, Navy Records.

86. George W. Dalzell, *The Flight from the Flag* (Chapel Hill, 1940), pp. 237–56.

87. Robert G. Albion and Jennie B. Pope, *Sea Lanes in Wartime the American Experience 1775–1942* (New York, 1942), p. 150, (hereinafter, Albion, *Sea Lanes in Wartime*).

CHAPTER SEVEN

1. Thomas F. Wilson to J. Watson Webb, Oct. 31, 1864, C. D. Bahia, Vol. III.

2. Log of the *Wachusett,* Oct. 4, 1864, Navy Records.

3. Morris to Barron, Oct. 13, 1864, *ORN,* Series I, III, 631.

4. Wilson to Webb, Oct. 31, 1864, C. D. Bahia, Vol. III.

5. Morris to Barron, Oct. 13, 1864, *ORN,* Series I, III, 631–2.

6. Wilson to Seward, Dec. 27, 1864, C. D. Bahia, Vol. III.

7. Morris to Barron, Oct. 13, 1864, *ORN,* Series I, III, 631–2.

8. Wilson to Webb, Oct. 31, 1864, C. D. Bahia, Vol. III.

9. Collins to Welles, Oct. 31, 1864, Commanders Letters, Vol. October–December 1864, IV.

10. Porter to Morris, Feb. 20, 1864, *ORN,* Series I, III, 637.

11. Collins to Welles, Oct. 31, 1864, Commanders Letters, Vol. October–December 1864, IV.

12. Log of the *Wachusett,* Oct. 7, 1864, Navy Records.

13. Collins to Welles, Oct. 31, 1864, Commanders Letters, Vol. October–December 1864, IV.

14. *Id.* to *id.,* Nov. 4, 1864, Commanders Letters, Vol. October–December 1864, IV.

15. *Id.* to *id.,* Nov. 14, 1864, Commanders Letters, Vol. October–December 1864, IV.

16. Wilson to Seward, Nov. 14, 1864, C. D. Bahia, Vol. III.

17. *Journal da Bahia,* Brazil, Oct. 11, 1864, enclosure in Webb to Seward, Oct. 19, 1864, L. D. Brazil, Vol. XXX.

18. Morris to Barron, Oct. 13, 1864, *ORN,* Series I, IV, 631–3.

19. Report of Gervasio Macebo, Oct. 7, 1864, enclosure in Ignacio de Avellar Barloza da Silva to Seward, Dec. 12, 1864, Notes from the Legation of Brazil, Vol. IV, State Department, Record Group 59, National Archives, Washington, D.C.

20. Preble to Welles, Mar. 1, 1864, and Collins to Welles, Nov. 17, 1864, Commanders Letters, Vol. October–December 1864, IV ; and Wilson to Webb, Oct. 31, 1864, C. D. Bahia, III ; and *ORN,* Series II, I, 235 and 252.

21. Log of the *Wachusett,* Oct. 8–29, 1864, Navy Records.

22. Collins to Welles, Nov. 14, 1864, Commanders Letters, Vol. October–December 1864, IV.

23. L. A. Beardslee to Collins, Oct. 31, 1864, Commanders Letters, Vol. October–December 1864, IV.

24. Log of the *Wachusett,* Oct. 30–31, 1864, Navy Records.

25. Porter to Morris, Feb. 20, 1865, *ORN,* Series I, III, 638.

26. Log of the *Wachusett,* Nov. 1, 1864, Navy Records.

27. Collins to Welles, Dec. 25, 1864, Commanders Letters, Vol. October–December 1864, IV.

28. John C. Edgar to Seward, Nov. 14, 1864, C. D. St. Thomas, Vol. VIII.

29. Log of the *Wachusett,* Nov. 2–12, 1864, Navy Records.

30. Porter to Morris, Feb. 20, 1865, *ORN,* Series I, III, 637–40.

31. Welles to H. A. Allen, Feb. 1, 1865, *ORN,* Series I, III, 288.

32. Court Martial Records, Vol. CLIX, 1864, number 4323, Case of the *Florida* aboard the U.S.S. *Colorado,* Hampton Roads, Dec. 6–12, 1864, Navy Records, Record Group 45, National Archives, Washington, D.C., (hereinafter, Court Martial Records, *Florida*).

33. David D. Porter to Jonathan Baker, Nov. 24, 1864, Court Martial Records, *Florida,* Navy Records.

34. David D. Porter to Welles, Nov. 28, 1864, *ORN,* Series I, III, 276.

35. Court Martial Records, *Florida,* Navy Records.

36. Undated note in Maffitt Papers.

37. David D. Porter, *Naval History of the Civil War* (New York, 1886), p. 816.

38.   Collins to Welles, Dec. 16, 1864, Commanders Letters, Vol. October–December 1864, IV.

39.   Webb to Seward, Oct. 18, 1864, L. D. Brazil, Vol. XXX.

40.   *Id.* to *id.*, May 23, 1863, L. D. Brazil, Vol. XXVIII.

41.   Seward to Webb, July 13, 1863, Instructions to Brazil, Vol. XVI.

42.   *Id.* to *id.*, Dec. 20, 1864, Instructions to Brazil, Vol. XVI.

43.   *Colburn's United Service Magazine and Naval and Military Journal,* Vol. CCCXXXIII (December, 1864), p. 604.

44.   John Slidell to J. P. Benjamin, Dec. 13, 1864, Post Records London.

45.   Barloza to Seward, Dec. 12, 1864, *ORN,* Series I, III, 283–5.

46.   Seward to Barloza, Dec. 26, 1864, Notes to the Brazilian Legation, Vol. VI, State Department, Record Group 59, National Archives, Washington, D.C.

47.   F. B. Blake to S. W. Gordon, July 25, 1866, *ORN,* Series I, III, 291–2.

48.   Wilson to Seward, Dec. 31, 1864, C. D. Bahia, Vol. III.

49.   Extract of the Court Martial of Commander Collins, U.S. Navy, *ORN,* Series I, III, 268–9.

50.   Welles to Collins, Sept. 17, 1866, *ORN,* Series I, III, 269.

51.   *Id.* to *id.*, May 18, 1863, and Collins to Welles, July 5, 1863, *ORN,* Series I, I, 598–9.

52.   Note by Compilers, *ORN,* Series I, III, 636.

53.   Richard Taylor to Morris, Oct. 8, 1864, *ORN,* Series I, III, 636.

54.   Barron to Morris, Nov. 10, 1864, *ORN,* Series I, III, 641–2.

55.   *Id.* to *id.*, Dec. 2, 1864, *ORN,* Series I, III, 642.

56.   Bulloch to G. S. Shyrock, Jan. 9, 1865, *ORN,* Series I, III, 729.

57.   Dudley to H. J. Perry, *ORN,* Series I, III, 446.

58.   Seward to Adams, Mar. 22, 1865, Post Records London.

59.   Portions of this chapter have appeared in Frank L. Owsley, Jr., "The Capture of the *CSS Florida,*" *The American Neptune,* XXII, pp. 45–54 (January, 1962).

CHAPTER EIGHT

1.   E. B. Potter (ed.), *The United States and World Sea Power* (Englewood Cliffs, New Jersey, 1955), p. 311.

2.   George W. Dalzell in *The Flight from the Flag* has an excel-

lent and detailed account of this process. See also, Albion, *Sea Lanes in Wartime,* pp. 150, 153.

 3. Dalzell, *The Flight from the Flag,* pp. 231–6; and Albion, *Sea Lanes in Wartime,* pp. 148–75.

 4. *Daily Register* (Mobile), May 4, 1886.

 5. *ORN,* Series II, I, 253.

 6. Albion, *Sea Lanes in Wartime,* p. 172.

 7. *Ibid.,* pp. 148–73.

 8. Dalzell, *The Flight from the Flag,* pp. 237–48; Owsley, *King Cotton Diplomacy,* pp. 554–5; *New York World,* July 7, 1864; Albion, *Sea Lanes in Wartime,* pp. 148–73.

Appendix A

Ships Captured by the *Florida* and her "Outfits"

CAPTURES MADE DURING THE "FLORIDA'S" FIRST CRUISE

Name of ship	Type	Date of Capture	Disposition
Estelle	Brig	Jan. 19, 1863	Burned
Windward	Brig	Jan. 22, 1863	Burned
Corris Ann	Brig	Jan. 22, 1863	Burned
Jacob Bell	Clipper Ship	Feb. 12, 1863	Burned
Star of Peace	Clipper Ship	Mar. 6, 1863	Burned
Aldabaran	Schooner	Mar. 12, 1863	Burned
Lapwing	Bark	Mar. 28, 1863	Used as a tender—eventually burned
M. J. Colcord	Bark	Mar. 30, 1863	Burned
Commonwealth	Clipper Ship	Apr. 17, 1863	Burned
Henrietta	Bark	Apr. 23, 1863	Burned
Oneida	Clipper Ship	Apr. 25, 1863	Burned
Clarence	Brig	May 6, 1863	Used as a raider—eventually burned
Crown Point	Clipper Ship	May 14, 1863	Burned
Kate Dyer	Clipper Ship	Apr. 20, 1863	Captured and bonded by the *Lapwing*

187

Name of ship	Type	Date of Capture	Disposition
Southern Cross	Clipper Ship	June 6, 1863	Burned
Red Gauntlet	Clipper Ship	June 14, 1863	Burned
Benjamin F. Hoxie	Clipper Ship	June 16, 1863	Burned
V. H. Hill	Schooner	June 27, 1863	Bonded
Sunrise	Clipper Ship	July 7, 1863	Bonded
W. B. Nash	Brig	July 8, 1863	Burned
Rienzi	Schooner	July 8, 1863	Burned
Francis B. Cutting	Clipper Ship	Aug. 6, 1863	Bonded
Southern Rights	Clipper Ship	Aug. 6, 1863	Bonded
Anglo Saxon	Clipper Ship	Aug. 21, 1863	Burned

CAPTURES MADE DURING THE "FLORIDA'S" SECOND CRUISE

Name of ship	Type	Date of Capture	Disposition
Avon	Clipper Ship	Mar. 29, 1864	Burned
George Latimer	Schooner	May 18, 1864	Burned
W. C. Clarke	Brig	June 17, 1864	Burned
Harriet Stevens	Bark	July 1, 1864	Burned
Golconda	Bark	July 8, 1864	Burned
Margaret Y. Davis	Schooner	July 9, 1864	Burned
Greenland	Bark	July 9, 1864	Burned
General Barry	Bark	July 10, 1864	Burned
Zelinda	Bark	July 10, 1864	Burned
Howard	Schooner	July 10, 1864	Bonded
Electric Spark (only steamer captured)	Steamer	July 10, 1864	Sunk by opening sea cocks and cutting pipes
Southern Rights	Clipper Ship	Aug. 22, 1864	Bonded
Mandamis	Bark	Sept. 26, 1864	Burned

CAPTURES MADE BY THE "CLARENCE" AND "TACONY"

Name of ship	Type	Date of Capture	Disposition
Whistling Wind	Bark	June 6, 1863	Burned
Mary Alvina	Bark	June 9, 1863	Burned
Tacony	Bark	June 12, 1863	Used as a raider and burned
M. A. Shindler	Schooner	June 12, 1863	Burned
Kate Stewart	Schooner	June 12, 1863	Bonded
Arabella	Brig	June 12, 1863	Bonded
Umpire	Brig	June 15, 1863	Burned
Isaac Webb	Clipper Ship	June 20, 1863	Bonded
Micawber	Fishing Schooner	June 20, 1863	Burned
Byzantium	Clipper Ship	June 21, 1863	Burned
Goodspeed	Bark	June 21, 1863	Burned
Marengo	Fishing Schooner	June 22, 1863	Burned
Elizabeth Ann	Fishing Schooner	June 22, 1863	Burned
Rufus Choate	Fishing Schooner	June 22, 1863	Burned
Ripple	Fishing Schooner	June 22, 1863	Burned
Florence	Fishing Schooner	June 22, 1863	Bonded
Ada	Fishing Schooner	June 23, 1863	Burned
Wanderer	Fishing Schooner	June 23, 1863	Burned
Shatemuc	Clipper Ship	June 24, 1863	Bonded
Archer	Fishing Schooner	June 24, 1863	Used as a raider and recaptured
Caleb Cushing	Revenue Cutter	June 26, 1863	Burned

Appendix B

Armament of the *Florida* Compared with the *Wachusett.*

	Florida	*Wachusett*
Tonnage	700	1,023
Length	192 feet	201 1/3 feet
Beam	27 1/6 feet	33 11/12 feet
Average Speed	9½ knots	6 knots
Maximum Speed with Steam and Sail	12 (at time of capture)	11½
Engines	two horizontal direct acting	two horizontal back acting
Battery	2 7-inch Blakely Rifles	3 6.4-inch Parrott Rifles
	6 6-inch Blakely Rifles	2 4.2-inch Parrott Rifles
	1 12-pound howitzer	4 32-pound smooth bore guns
		1 12-pound rifle
Total Broadside	360 pounds	320 pounds
Builder	W. C. Miller & Sons Liverpool England	Boston Navy Yard
Class	screw steamer	screw steamer
Hull	wood	wood

Bibliography

UNPUBLISHED PRIVATE MANUSCRIPTS AND PUBLIC DOCUMENTS

British Public Record Office, London

British Foreign Office Papers
Diplomatic Correspondence
F.O. 5, Vols. MCCCXIII and MCCCXIV, Papers relating to
the Confederate Cruiser *Florida*

National Archives, Washington, D.C.

Record Group 45—Navy Records

1. Allotment Records of the *Florida*, November 1862—
   January 1863
2. Bryan, George D., Abstract of Log of the *Florida* and Log
   of the *Lapwing*
3. Confidential Letters Sent (Record of Confidential Letters)
4. Court Martial Records
5. Executive Letter Book (Secretary of the Navy)
6. Letters from Admirals, Commodores and Captains
7. Letters from Commanders
8. Letters from Officers Commanding Squadrons: West India
   Squadron and North Atlantic Blockading Squadron
9. Log of the *Florida* (August 17, 1862—June 1, 1863 ; January
   1—September 1864). There were several copies of the Log of
   the *Florida*, and as a result many of the dates are overlapping—see RG 76

191

10. Log of the *Kearsarge*
11. Log of the *Wachusett*
12. Miscellaneous Letters Received ("Miscellaneous Letters")
13. Miscellaneous Letters Sent
14. Payroll of allotments granted on board *CSS Florida* payable at the Naval Station at New Orleans, October 10, 1862.

Record Group 56—Treasury Records

Letterbook of Jedediah Jewett, Collector of Customs, Portland, Maine

Record Group 59—State Department Records

Consular Despatches

1. Bahia
2. Barbados
3. Bermuda
4. Havana
5. Liverpool
6. London
7. Nassau N. P.
8. Paris
9. Pernambuco
10. St. Thomas

Despatches from United States Legations

1. Brazil
2. France
3. Great Britain

Instructions from Secretary of State to United States Legations

1. Brazil
2. France
3. Great Britain

Official notes to and from foreign governments

1. Notes to the British Government
2. Notes from the Legation of Brazil

Record Group 76—State Department Records

Records relating to Civil War Claims United States and Great Britain

1. Journal of Midshipman C. C. Cary
2. Letterbook of Lt. Charles M. Morris
3. Log of the *Florida* (August 17, 1862—January 22, 1863 ; September 17—December 31, 1863 ; September 17, 1863— April 30, 1864 ; May 1—October 3, 1864)
4. Miscellaneous papers relating to the *Florida ;* including Register of the ship, statements of seamen and other papers
5. Sick Log of the *Florida*
6. Steam Log of the *Florida*

Record Group 84—State Department Records

Records of Foreign Posts of United States Legations

1. Britain
2. France

Sanford Memorial Library, Sanford, Florida

Henry Shelton Sanford Papers

*Southern Historical Collections,
University of North Carolina*

1. Buchanan-Screven Papers—Papers of Admiral Franklin Buchanan

194   *The C.S.S. Florida: Her Building and Operations*

2. John Newland Maffitt Papers—Collection of the Private Papers, Letters, Scrapbooks and Parts of the Journal of Commander Maffitt. (Maffitt's Journal as found in the Maffitt Collection is only a fragment of the entire journal. Additional parts are found in Emma Maffitt's *Life and Services of John Newland Maffitt* and additional material, perhaps a later edited copy, appears in the *ORN*. Overlapping fragments in the Maffitt Collection indicate that Maffitt made several accounts of his war activities. Since the differences in the accounts are a matter of greater or lesser detail, all three sources have been used in this work.)

3. Wilson, H. W., "Cruise of the Oneida," a manuscript diary.

University of Alabama Library

Rodimon, William. The Confederate Cruiser *Florida,* unpublished master's thesis, University of Alabama, 1939.

PRINTED PUBLIC DOCUMENTS

Civil War Naval Chronology 1861–1865. 5 vols. Washington: Government Printing Office, 1961–.

Correspondence Concerning Claims Against Great Britain transmitted to the Senate of the United States in Answer to the Resolution of December 4 and 10, 1867, and of May 27, 1868. 7 vols. Washington: Government Printing Office, 1869–71.

Lees, John Campbell. *Decree of His Honor John Campbell Lees, Esquire, Judge of the Vice-Admiralty Court of the Bahamas, in the Case of the British Steamship Oreto Seized for an Alleged Violation of the Foreign Enlistment Act. Delivered 2nd Day of August, A.D. 1862.* Nassau N.P.: The Nassau Guardian, 1862.

Official Records of the Union and Confederate Navies in the War of the Rebellion. 31 vols. Washington: Government Printing Office, 1894–1927.

Papers Relating to Foreign Affairs: Executive Documents Printed by Order of the House of Representatives During the Second Session of the Thirty-eighth Congress, 1863–64. 15 vols. Washington: Government Printing Office, 1865.

Register of Officers of the Confederate States Navy 1861–1865. Washington: Government Printing Office, 1931.

NEWSPAPERS

Daily Post, Liverpool, England
Daily Register, Mobile, Alabama
Journal Da Bahia, Bahia, Brazil
New York Times, New York, New York
New York World, New York, New York
Norwich Weekly Courier, Norwich, Connecticut
Post, Boston, Massachusetts
Royal Gazette, Hamilton, Bermuda
Times, London, England

BOOKS

Adams, Ephram Douglass. *Great Britain and the American Civil War.* 2 vols. New York: Russell and Russell, 1958.
Albion, Robert Greenhalgh, and Pope, Jennie Barnes. *Sea Lanes In Wartime: The American Experience 1775–1942.* New York: W. W. Norton, 1942.
Alexander, Roy. *The Cruise of the Raider "Wolf."* New Haven: Yale University Press, 1939.
Anderson, Bern. *By Sea and By River: The Naval History of the Civil War.* New York: Alfred A. Knopf, 1962.
Beaman, Charles C., Jr. *The National and Private "Alabama Claims" and Their "Final and Amicable Settlement."* Washington: W. H. Moore, 1871.
Bemis, Samuel Flagg. *A Short History of American Foreign Policy and Diplomacy.* New York: Holt, Rinehart & Winston, 1959.
Bigelow, John. *France and the Confederate Navy 1862–1868, an International Episode.* New York: Harper and Brothers, 1888.
Blumenthal, Henry. *France and the United States: Their Diplomatic Relations, 1789–1914.* New York: W. W. Norton, 1970.
Boykin, Edward. *Sea Devil of the Confederacy: The Story of the Florida and her Captain, John Newland Maffitt.* New York: Funk and Wagnalls, 1959.
Bradlee, Francis B. *Blockade Running During the Civil War and the Effect of Land and Water Transportation on the Confederacy.* Philadelphia: Porcupine Press, 1974.
Bulloch, James D. *The Secret Services of the Confederate States in Europe or How the Confederate Cruisers Were Equipped.* 2 vols. New York: Putnam's, 1883.

Burdick, Charles. *The Frustrated Raider: The Story of the German Cruiser Cormorna in World War I.* Carbondale: Southern Illinois University Press, 1979.

Callahan, James M. *Diplomatic History of the Southern Confederacy.* New York: F. Unger, 1964.

Carse, Robert. *Blockade, the Civil War at Sea.* New York and Toronto: Rinehart, 1958.

Case, Lynn M., and Spencer, Warren F. *The United States and France: Civil War Diplomacy.* Philadelphia: University of Pennsylvania Press, 1970.

Cochran, Hamilton. *Blockade Runners of the Confederacy.* Indianapolis: Bobbs-Merrill, 1958.

Coletta, Paolo E. *American Secretaries of the Navy.* 2 vols. Annapolis: Naval Institute Press, 1980.

Cook, Adrian. *The Alabama Claims, American Politics and Anglo American Relations, 1865–1872.* Ithaca: Cornell University Press, 1975.

Coulter, E. Merton. *The Confederate States of America 1861–1865.* Baton Rouge: Louisiana State University Press, 1950.

Dalzell, George W. *The Flight from the Flag.* Chapel Hill: University of North Carolina Press, 1940.

Davis, Charles S. *Colin J. McRae: Confederate Financial Agent.* Tuscaloosa, Ala.: Confederate Publishing, 1961.

Delaney, Norman C. *John McIntosh Kell of the Raider Alabama.* University: University of Alabama Press, 1973.

Durkin, Joseph T. *Stephen R. Mallory: Confederate Navy Chief.* Chapel Hill: University of North Carolina Press, 1954.

Evans, Clement A. *Confederate Military History.* 12 vols. Atlanta: Confederate Publishing, 1899.

Forrest, Douglas French, C.S.N. *Oddyssey in Gray: A Diary of Confederate Service 1863–1865.* William N. Still, Jr., ed. Richmond: Virginia State Library, 1979.

Hagen, Kenneth J., ed. *In Peace and War: Interpretations of American Naval History 1775–1984.* 2nd ed. Westport, Conn.: Greenwood Press, 1984.

Hill, Jim Dan. *Sea Dogs of the Sixties; Farragut and Seven Contemporaries.* Minneapolis: University of Minnesota Press, 1935.

Hendrick, Burton J. *Statesmen of the Lost Cause: Jefferson Davis and His Cabinet.* Boston: Little, Brown, 1939.

Hoole, William Stanley. *Four Years in the Confederate Navy.* Athens: University of Georgia Press, 1964.

————, ed. *Confederate Foreign Agent: The European Diary of Major Edward C. Anderson.* University, Ala.: Confederate Publishing, 1976.

Horan, James D., ed. *C.S.S. Shenandoah: The Memoirs of Lieutenant Commanding James I. Waddell.* New York: Crown Publishers, 1960.

Hoyt, Edwin P. *The Phantom Raider.* New York: Thomas Y. Crowell, 1969.

Jenkins, Brian. *Britain and the War for the Union.* 2 vols. Montreal: McGill-Queen's University Press, 1974 and 1980.

Jones, Wilbur Devereux. *The Confederate Rams at Birkenhead: A Chapter in Anglo American Relations.* Tuscaloosa, Ala.: Confederate Publishing, 1961.

Jones, Virgil C. *The Civil War at Sea.* 3 vols. New York: Holt, 1960–62.

Lester, Richard I. *Confederate Finance and Purchasing in Great Britain.* Charlottesville: University Press of Virginia, 1975.

Macartney, Clarence Edward. *Mr. Lincoln's Admirals.* New York: Funk & Wagnalls, 1956.

MaClay, Edgar Stanton. *A History of the United States Navy from 1775 to 1898.* 3 vols. New York: D. Appleton, 1893.

Merrill, James J. *The Rebel Shore, the Story of Union Seapower in the Civil War.* Boston: Little, Brown, 1957.

Merli, Frank J. *Great Britain and the Confederate Navy, 1861–1865.* Bloomington: Indiana University Press, 1970.

Owsley, Frank L. *King Cotton Diplomacy Foreign Relations of the Confederate States of America.* 2nd ed. Chicago: University of Chicago Press, 1959.

Porter, David D. *Naval History of the Civil War.* New York: Sherman Publishing, 1886.

Potter, E. B., ed. *The United States and World Sea Power.* Englewood Cliffs, N.J.: Prentice-Hall, 1955.

Robinson, William M., Jr. *The Confederate Privateers.* New Haven: Yale University Press, 1928.

Scharf, J. Thomas. *History of the Confederate States Navy from its Organization to the Surrender of its Last Vessel.* Albany: Joseph McDonough, 1894.

Semmes, Raphael. *Service Afloat or the Remarkable Career of the Confederate Cruisers Sumpter and Alabama during the War Between the States.* New York: P. J. Kennedy, n.d. (1869 circa).

Smith, Myron J. *American Civil War Navies: A Bibliography.* Metuchen, N.J.: Scarecrow Press, 1972.

Soley, James Russell. *The Navy in the Civil War.* Vol. I, *The Blockade and the Cruisers.* New York: Charles Scribner's Sons, 1883.

Spencer, Warren F. *The Confederate Navy in Europe.* University: University of Alabama Press, 1983.

Sprout, Harold, and Sprout, Margaret. *The Rise of American Naval Power 1776–1918.* Princeton: Princeton University Press, 1946.

Stern, Philip Van Doren. *When Guns Roared: World Aspects of the American Civil War.* Garden City, N.Y.: Doubleday, 1965.

Still, William N., Jr. *Confederate Shipbuilding.* Athens: University of Georgia Press, 1969.

Summersell, Charles G. *The Cruise of C.S.S. Sumter.* Tuscaloosa, Ala.: Confederate Publishing, 1965.

———. *The Journal of George Townley Fullam, Boarding Officer of the Confederate Sea Raider Alabama.* University: University of Alabama Press, 1973.

———. *CSS Alabama: Builder, Captain, and Plans.* University: University of Alabama Press, 1985.

Thomas, Lowell. *Count Luckner the Sea Devil.* Garden City: Doubleday, Doran, 1929.

Thompson, Robert M. *Confidential Correspondence of Gustavus V. Fox.* 2 vols. New York: Naval History Society, 1928.

Weems, Bob. *Charles Read Confederate Bucaneer.* Jackson, Miss.: Heritage Books, 1982.

Welles, Gideon. *Diary of Gideon Welles, Secretary of the Navy Under Lincoln and Johnson.* 3 vols. Boston: Houghton Mifflin, 1911.

West, Richard S., Jr. *Gideon Welles, Lincoln's Navy Department.* Indianapolis: Bobbs-Merrill, 1943.

———. *Mr. Lincoln's Navy.* New York: Longman's Green, 1958.

U.S. Navy Department, *Civil War Naval Chronology 1861–1865.* Washington: Government Printing Office, 1971.

Van Der Vat, Dan. *The Last Corsair: The Story of the Emden.* London: Hodder and Stoughton, 1983.

ARTICLES

Andrew, Christopher. "The Affair of the Weighted Canvas Bag That Didn't Sink," *The Listener,* 115 (January 2, 1986).

Anonymous. "Editorial," *Colburn's United Service Magazine and Naval and Military Journal,* 433 (December 1864).

Fessenden, B. L. "The Yankee Clipper and the Cape Cod Bay," *American Neptune,* 23 (October 1964).

Lawson, Raymond S. "It Happened in Bahia," *United States Naval Institute Proceedings,* 58 (June 1932).

Leary, William M., Jr. "The Alabama vs. The Kearsarge: A Diplomatic View," *American Neptune,* 29 (August 1969).

Maffitt, John N. "Reminiscences of the Confederate Navy," *United Service,* 3 (October 1880).

Maynard, Douglas H. "The Escape of the *Florida,*" *Pennsylvania Magazine of History and Biography,* 77 (April 1953).

Merli, Frank J. "Crown Versus Cruiser, Curious Case of the *Alexandra,*" *Civil War History,* 2 (June 1963).

Morgan, James M. "The Confederate Cruiser *Florida,*" *United States Naval Institute Proceedings,* 42 (September–October 1916).

Owsley, Frank L. "The Capture of the C.S.S. *Florida,*" *American Neptune,* 22 (January 1962).

————. "The C.S.S. *Florida's* Tour de Force at Mobile Bay," *The Alabama Review,* 15 (October 1962).

Porter, Thomas K. "Capture of the Confederate Steamer *Florida,*" *Southern Historical Society Papers,* 12 (January 1884).

Sinclair, G. Terry (pseudonym for Tennie Mathews, Jr.). "The Eventful Cruise of the *Florida,*" *The Century Magazine,* 56 (July 1898).

Smith, Myron J. "Mystic Treasure Ship of the Civil War," *Log of Mystic Seaport,* 20 (June 1968).

Soley, James Russell. "The Confederate Cruisers," *Battles and Leaders of the Civil War,* 4 (1888).

Index

Maffitt at Mobile, 44–45, at
  Brest, 102–103
Barrett, R. H., 36, 43
Barron, Samuel, 139
Barron, Lt. Samuel, Jr., 155
Battle of Gettysburg, 163
Bayley, Gov. C. J., 25, 27–30, 52
Bayman, Consul Robert, 114
Beardslee, L. A., 140, 143, 145
Belle Isle, 97, 111, 113
Benjamin F. Hoxie, the, captured
  by *Florida,* 71–72
Benjamin, Judah P., 184f
Bermuda, 27, 71, 74–75, 116,
  118–120, 122–23, 125, 146, 157
Bermuda, the, 23
Bigelow, Consul John, 93–95
Blake, F. B., 184f
Blunt, George W., 181f
Boston, Mass., 50, 58, 70, 80,
  82–83, 85, 115, 120, 147
Bourne, John T., 71
Bradford, Passed Master O.,
  joins *Florida,* 31, leaves
  Florida, 46
Brazil, 64, 66, 118, 123
Brest, France, 69, 75–77, 92–93,
  95–99, 101, 103–106, 108, 110–
  111, 120, 157–58
Bridgetown, Barbados, *Florida*
  in port, 55–57
Brooklyn, U.S.S., 48
Brown, Engineer E. H., 79, 88
Brown, George T., 171f
Brown, Captain John, 50
Brown, Engineer John B., joins
  Florida, 122
Brunswick, Maine, 127
Bryan, Midshipman George D.,
  168f
Buchanan, Admiral Franklin,
  42–44, 47
Bulldog, H.M.S., 25

Bulloch, James D., efforts to
  obtain ships in Britain, 17–21,
  23–24, 30–31, 63, 100, 123
Burwell's Bay, 79
Butler, Fireman James, 124
Byzantium, the, captured by
  Tacony, 82

Cabot, Stephen, 181f
Cadiz, Spain, 108–109, 111, 116
Calais, France, 108
Caleb Cushing, the, captured by
  C. W. Read, 88–89, 91
California, 47, 117
California steamer, 117
Camp Lincoln, 89
Cape of Good Hope, 118
Capes of the Chesapeake, 79
Capetown, South Africa, 62
Cardenas, Cuba, 36, 52, 82
Carey, Captain, 71
Cary, C. C., 181f
Castelbrance, Gov. Joaquin
  Pedro de, 114
Ceara, Brazil, 70
Charleston, S. C., 17, 32, 57
Charlton, Surgeon T. J., 103,
  117–119, 146
Chase, Salmon P., 175f
Cherbourg, France, 107
Chesapeake Bay, 79
Chesapeake, the, 89–90
Christian, the, 62
Clarence, the, captured by
  Florida, 63, 65, 77–79, 81, 87
*Colburn's United Service Maga-
  zine,* 152
Collier, Engineer Charles H.,
  123–24
Collins, Napoleon, 137, 139–46,
  150–51, 153–54
Commonwealth, the, captured by
  Florida, 62, 64

at Nassau, 52–53, chased by *Sonoma*, 53–54, at Bridgetown, Barbados, 55–57, engineering difficulties, 58, impact of captures, 59, 61–62, at Fernando de Noronha, 63, 66, 69–76, enters port at Brest, 77, 78, 86–87, repairs, 92–93, seized, 94–95, not considered a privateer, 95–96, repairs to guns, 97–98, discharge of crew, 98–101, new crew, 101–102, C. M. Morris takes command, 102–103, hauled out of drydock, 105–108, put to sea, 108–109, ship's speed, 110, receives contraband, 111, at Funchal, Madeira, 112–114, at Santa Cruz, Tenerife, 115, at Saint-Pierre, Martinique, 116–18, exchanges salute with H.M.S. *Nimble*, 118, engineering difficulties, 118–20, repairs at St. Georges, Bermuda, 121–25, coastal raid, 127–33, captures *Electric Spark* (only steamer), 129–32, at Santa Cruz, Tenerife, 133, mutiny of part of crew, 134–35, arrival at Bahia and end of cruise, 135–37, permitted to repair at Bahia, 138–39, attacked and captured, 140–44, taken to Hampton Roads, 145–48, sunk, 148–51, reaction to capture, 152–54, 155, 156, difficulty in obtaining coal, 157–58, effect of raids, 159–63
Forest City, the, 89–91
Forrest, Lt. Dulany A., 46
Forster, Henry, and Co., 172f
Fort Morgan, 37, 40
Fort Preble, 89, 91

Fort Warren, 147
Fortress Monroe, 79–80, 127, 147
Fox, G. V., 130
Francis B. Cutting, the, captured by *Florida*, 75
Francis Milly, the, 115
Fraser, Trenholm and Co., principal commercial representative of Confederacy in England, 17–18, 22, 71, 100, 123
French Minister of Marine, 94
Frisbie, Captain, captain of *Jacob Bell*, 55
Funchal Roads, 112–15, 157

Gaines, C.S.S., 48
Gansevoort, Guert, 167f
Garretson, F. (see also Van Biber), 43
General Barry, the, captured by *Florida*, 127
George Channing, the, 113
George Latimer, the, captured by *Florida*, 120
Georgia, C.S.S., 98, 107–109
Gibraltar, 24
Gill, Thomas, 24
Glisson, O. S., 64
Gomez Leal, Col. Antonio, 63
Golconda, the, captured by *Florida*, 126
Goodspeed, the, captured by *Tacony*, 82
Gordon, S. W., 181f
Grafton, Assistant Surgeon J. D., drowned, 69
Grand Banks, 85
Grange, the, 152–53
Green Cay, 33
Greenland, the, captured by *Florida*, 126–27
Green Turtle Cay, 154
Greyhound, H.M.S., 26

Greyhound (blockade runner), 124

guerilla warfare, 159

guerre de course, guerilla warfare of the sea, 5, 159

Gulf of Mexico, 123

Halifax, Nova Scotia, 27, 87

Halkier, Fireman James, 148–49

Hamilton, Bermuda, 71

Hamilton *Royal Gazette,* 71

Hampton Roads, 63, 78–80, 147–48, 153

Hand, Captain, 58

Harriet Stevens, the, captured by *Florida,* 124

Harve de Grace, Md., 86

Harvey, James E., U.S. Minister to Portugal, 114

Havana, Cuba, 26, 36–37, 51–52

Helm, Maj. Charles, 51

Henrietta, the, captured by *Florida,* 62

Hinckley, Comm. H. D., 26–29

Hitchcock, R. B., 169f

Hog Island, 32

Hong Kong, 70

Hoole, Lt. J. S., joined *Florida,* 46, 55, left *Florida,* 116–18

Hope, Vice Admiral James, 121

Howard, the, captured by *Florida,* 127

Howlands Islands, 115

Hudson, James, 165f

Hull, F. S., advised Bulloch on legal status of *Florida,* 20

Huntress, C.S.S., 103

Hyland, W. C. J., 173f

Inland Island, 122

Iroquois, U.S.S., 118

Isaac Webb, the, captured by *Tacony,* 82

Italian Consul, 21

Jackson, W. H., third assistant engineer on *Florida* during first cruise, 58

Jackson, W. H., engineer on second cruise (not believed to be same Jackson as one on first cruise), 124–25, 128, 133

Jacob Bell, the, captured by *Florida,* 54–55, 59, 64

Jewett, Jedediah, 89–90

Kate Dyer, the, captured by *Lapwing,* 68–69

Kate Stewart, the, captured by *Clarence,* 81, 87

Kearsarge, U.S.S., watches *Florida* at Brest, 104–109, 111, 146, 160

Kennebunk River, 131

Key West, Florida, 81

King, Surgeon M., 140

Klawillen, the, 135

Lake, Engineer J. C., relieved from duty, 117, discharged, 119

Lane, the, 128

Lannau, William, 147–49

Lapwing, the, captured and "outfitted" by *Florida,* 61–63, 67–70, 77–78

Lardner, James L., 117–18

Laura Ann, the, 59

Lee, S. P., 175f

Lees, Judge W. C., 29

L'Embuscade, the, 152

Le Roy, the, 87

Lillian, the, 124

Lincoln, Abraham, 57, 70

Lisbon, Portugal, 112

Liverpool, England, 17, 19, 71–

ABOUT THE AUTHOR

Frank Lawrence Owsley, Jr., Professor Emeritus of History, Auburn University, taught naval history for several years at the United States Naval Academy. He has written extensively in the fields of naval and military history, including *Struggle for the Gulf Borderlands: The Creek War and the Battle of New Orleans, 1812–1815,* and *Filibusters and Expansionists: Jeffersonian Manifest Destiny, 1800–1821.* He received his B.A. degree from Vanderbilt and his M.A. and Ph.D. degrees from The University of Alabama.